THE POW WHO SAVED KASHMIR

Unsung Saga of Sher Bachha Brig Pritam Singh, MC

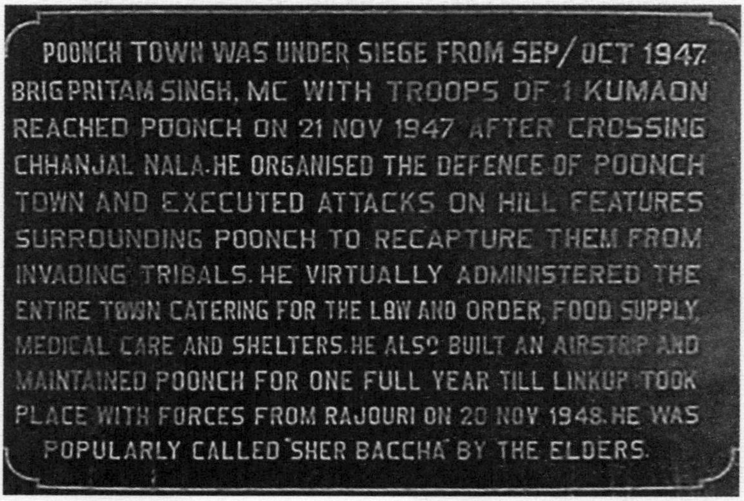

An inscription in Poonch town

THE POW WHO SAVED KASHMIR

Unsung Saga of Sher Bachha Brig Pritam Singh, MC

Brigadier Jasbir Singh, SM

Pankaj P Singh

THE BROWSER | FAUJI DAYS

Title: The POW Who Saved Kashmir
Unsung Saga of Sher Bacha Brig Pritam Singh, MC
Author: Brigadier Jasbir Singh, SM & Pankaj P Singh

ISBN: 978-93-92210-26-6
Edition: 3

Published by:
J.G.S. Enterprises Pvt Ltd
Imprint: The Browser

Publisher's Address:
SCO 14-15, FF, Sector 8-C, Chandigarh 160 009

Website: www.thebrowser.org
Email: service@thebrowser.org

First published by The Browser in 2020
This edition published by The Browser in 2023
Printed in India

THE BROWSER
www.thebrowser.org
Publishers & Booksellers

FAUJI DAYS
www.faujidays.com
Oral History and Military Publishing

Contents

Foreword

Fifteen years ago, I found myself standing on a deserted parade ground with my father in Clement Town in Dehradun. There were some dilapidated barracks nearby that during the Second World War had housed Italian PoWs and subsequently were home to the first batches of the Joint Services Wing, the forebear of the National Defence Academy. My father, Major General Ashok Kalyan Verma, at that point of time, had hung up his boots more than a decade ago. He was from 8 JSW from where he had then moved to the Indian Military Academy in 1955.

My father was uncharacteristically quiet, the sound of hobnailed boots and the voice of *ustaads* long gone echoing in his head. The light was fading quickly, and in the enveloping darkness, I finally asked him, "At what point did you decide to join the Army?" Without a moments' hesitation, he said, "1948. We had just joined Birla Mandir (Nainital . . . where he would go on to be the first Head Boy) when in the School Assembly the Principal announced that the Indian Air Force in the early morning hours had landed 25-pounders at Poonch. The town had been under siege for months and was desperately fighting for survival under Brigadier Pritam Singh. All the boys started to cheer . . . some were crying, for we were through All India Radio fully aware of what was happening . . . it was like a flash in my head . . . I just knew it was going to be the Army for me. It was as clear as that."

Poonch . . . Jhangar . . . Naushera . . . 50 Parachute Brigade . . . Baba Mehar Singh . . . Brigadier Pritam Singh . . . it was like a cauldron in my head. I had first heard the stories from my father, and later, one fiendishly devoured whatever information one could find on these subjects. Bogey Sen's Slender was the Thread and Eric Vas's *Without Baggage* became constant reading companions, as did, surprisingly, the Ministry of Defence's *Official History of the J&K Ops* written by SN Prasad, one of the most outstanding pieces of work that meticulously documented the fighting in the period immediately after independence.

In 1995 I was making a film on the history of the Indian Army, that until then mostly centred around events in Jammu and Kashmir. It was but a matter of time before we found ourselves in Poonch. The task was to recreate some of the events that had taken place during the desperate months in early 1948. Given the general Indian apathy and indifference towards military history, there was very little information on the events themselves, let alone details about the key people involved. However, as one talked to the local *Poonchies* who had lived through the dark, uncertain days, Brigadier Pritam Singh's name cropped up regularly. These were the pre-internet days, and I searched in vain for more details about this remarkable man but mostly drew a blank. Years later, while visiting Major General (later Lieutenant General) Khonsom Himalay Singh, who was commanding the Rajauri based 25 Infantry Division, I was told the Army had commissioned a painting of the "aviour of Poonch." I immediately set off with KH for the Divisional Museum and photographed the extremely well-done portrait of the man who had not only held the Poonch Valley against difficult odds but had also kept the morale of the people high.

The story of the raiding parties that set out to get food for the besieged garrison was scripted into the film, and I filmed the scenes across the Betar Nullah, much to the consternation of the Pakistanis. Radio intercepts that evening had us in splits as the local Pakistani posts were reporting on our little film shoot as a "major military build-up". Radio Pakistan also gravely announced in its Urdu News that serious steps were being taken by the Indians in the Poonch Sector . . . for what exactly, they did not say.

Brigadier Pritam's contribution to India's first conflict post-independence needs to be understood in its totality. 1 Kumaon, along with 1 Sikh and 4 Kumaon, were among the first troops to be airlifted into the Valley towards the end of October 1947. The battle of Shalateng, fought by a handful of troops against a vastly larger force, decisively broke the back of the tribal *lashkar* that was heading for Srinagar. As the commanding officer of 1 Kumaon, Pritam was asked to head from Uri along the Hyderabad Nullah and link up with the State Forces that were holding out at Poonch. The surrounding heights were entirely held by Pakistani forces and had the move been abandoned, no one would have raised an eyebrow, for the terrain that links Uri to Poonch through Haji Pir is a defending force's delight. The courage and determination displayed by 1 Kumaon to effect the link-up speaks volumes for their commanding officer.

The subsequent year-long siege, described in this book in detail, needs to be recognised for what it was. It perhaps suffices to remember that if Pritam had not done what he did, the fate of not just Poonch but even Srinagar earlier, would have been a hundred times worse than that of Mirpur where 400 women had to jump into a well to save themselves from being ravaged by the tribesmen.

Petty politics later led to not just Pritam Singh's name being blackened, and even others like Group Captain "Baba" Mehar

Singh were not spared by those with clear, vested interests. Now, nearly seven-and-a-half decades later, it is perhaps time for India to look into this grave injustice of history and recognise a valiant son for having stood firm and having done his duty. This book quotes from Monty Palit's records to clear Pritam's name, and I have had a long discussion with him on this subject while researching for my own books. Most importantly, any person from Poonch who was from that generation who had come into contact with Pritam Singh simply eulogised the "Sher Bachha". Respect, they say, cannot be bought, it can only be earned. Brigadier Pritam Singh needs to be remembered for what he was . . . a true soldier!

This book has long been overdue. But justice delayed is better than no justice at all. It is time India not only recognises the man for what he did, but his story must also become a part of folklore. In 1948 it had a profound impact on my father and his generation. There is no reason why it should no longer continue to do so.

Shiv Kunal Verma
November 2019
Gurgaon

Author's Note

—Brig Jasbir Singh, SM

> It doesn't take a hero to order men into battle. It takes a hero to be one of those men who goes into battle.
>
> —*General Norman Schwarzkopf*

This book recounts the saga of patriotism and courage of a brave soldier of the Indian Army (IA)—Brigadier Pritam Singh, MC.

Pritam's legendary exploits have greatly influenced the history of Jammu and Kashmir (J&K) earning him the honorific title of Sher Bachha of Poonch. He was a rare human being with all the qualities of a great soldier and leader which drew other valiant soldiers to his side. He performed incredible deeds of gallantry during a military career that spanned World War II and the First Kashmir War of 1947–48.

During the Battle of Singapore in World War II, Pritam was seriously wounded in a Japanese air attack and could barely survive. He was taken prisoner by the Japanese and then thrown into a prisoner-of-war (POW) camp in Singapore. The gutsy Pritam escaped from there along with two other officers of IA—Captains Balbir Singh and GS Parab. The trio reached India after a daring and long journey, passing through enemy-held lands of Malaya, Thailand and Burma.

Back in active service, Pritam did parachute jumps to earn his parachute wings, and on 30 October 1947 assumed command of 1 Kumaon (Para). The next morning, he flew with his unit to Srinagar to fight the attacking tribal raiders who had been strengthened with Pakistan Army personnel and sent to annexe Kashmir for Pakistan. Leading his troops from the front, Pritam fought in the decisive Battle of Shalateng and caused the surviving raiders to flee, after nearly decimating them on the field. This battle was a significant one that changed the history of Kashmir, and Pritam, at the helm of 1 Kumaon (Para) chased the fleeing tribal raiders all the way to Uri. Once there, he came to know that the township of Poonch was under attack and likely to fall into the hands of the tribal *lashkars.* Pritam was ordered to divert his move and advance with haste to reach Poonch via Haji Pir.

Though the enemy attempted to stop Pritam by ambushing his unit and setting fire to a crucial wooden bridge on the way from Uri to Poonch, he surged ahead as a man possessed. He knew that terrible atrocities would be committed on the people of Poonch if the raiders managed to enter the township. Memories of the brutality perpetrated on the hapless people of Baramulla and nuns of the local convent and hospital there were fresh in his mind and spurred him and his relieving force. Fortunately, they reached Poonch just in time to save the civilian population from the raiders. The tribal lashkars from Pakistan were already deployed on the hills surrounding Poonch, ready to attack it any time.

When Pritam entered the town, he found that the two J&K State Forces battalions which had been defending the beleaguered township were ready to depart because of the attacks by the tribal *lashkars*. Pritam stopped the State Forces units from leaving Poonch, and instead motivated them to fight.

He remained besieged for a full year, during which time he repeatedly defeated the tribal invaders and kept them at bay.

It was a historic defence of Poonch. On 6 December 1947, he handed over command of 1 Kumaon (Para) to his second-in-command, Lieutenant Colonel Dharam Singh. He was promoted to the rank of a Brigadier and assumed command of the garrison at Poonch.

Pritam's feats in beating back enemy attacks while being besieged in Poonch deserve to find a place of honour in the annals of modern military history. During the year-long siege, Pritam repeatedly hit the raiders and saved the township and its surrounding heights for India. Severely injured in Poonch, some people even believed that he had died of his wounds. But he miraculously survived and kept up the brave fight.

Once the raiders were beaten, he attempted a link-up with the Indian forces under Brigadier Yadunath Singh, who had meanwhile advanced from Jammu. The first attempt failed, but the second was successful, and the link-up took place.

Although Poonch was now safe, sadly, events took an unexpected turn for the worse for the hero. Pritam was ostracised for minor administrative infringements, disgraced and removed from command of the Brigade at Poonch. The tragic circumstances did not end there and even his medals were confiscated. However, much as they may have wanted to, the ungrateful authorities could not confiscate the Military Cross and medals of World War II that had been awarded by the British government. Professional jealousies had come to the fore, and Pritam's monumentally courageous deeds were quickly forgotten.

He was not given any recognition for the gallant work of saving Poonch for India. The poetic epithet says it all:

Faced with a crisis or when war clouds loom,
Gallant soldiers rise up to banish the gloom,
Once the crisis is over, and conditions are righted,
Soldiers are forgotten and may even be slighted.

In his later years Brigadier Pritam Singh, MC, would say:

> "Sometimes serious doubts assail me, on whether it would have been better to let the State Forces garrison slip out of Poonch and merely follow them than to have put up that tenacious fight. But, I dispel the doubts with my conviction that I have done my duty to India and one day the truth will be out for all to see."

Grossly unfair treatment was meted out to him after all the outstanding deeds he had performed for Indian Army (IA) and India.

On reading this book, I hope that you, the reader, will agree that the brave exploits of Brigadier Pritam Singh, MC, need to be fairly honoured. His case must be reviewed to serve the ends of justice posthumously. Some years ago this forgotten hero of India died in the countryside of Punjab, a thoroughly disillusioned man. We owe it to posterity to urgently resurrect the memory of this brave-heart.

The first part of the book is the little-known story of the daring escape by Pritam, Balbir and Parab from a Japanese POW camp in Singapore. They undertook their journey through enemy-controlled areas for nearly six months by foot, elephants, rail, bus, boat and finally by air to reach India.

The gruelling journey took them across war-ravaged Malaya, and parts of Thailand and Burma. During the escape, the three officers had great adventures and also experienced many hardships, endured with courage and fortitude. The Japanese recaptured the officers on two occasions. After their capture at Monywa, they were physically tortured and interrogated in great detail. Despite the intense torture they underwent at the hands of the *Kempeitai* or Japanese Military Police, they convinced their captors that they were innocent civilians who had been displaced by the war. The *Kempeitai* believed their story, and they were finally released.

Captain (later Brigadier)
Pritam Singh, MC

Captain (later Brigadier)
Balbir Singh, MC

Captain (later Colonel)
GS Parab, MC

After their experience of Japanese brutality in Monywa, the group split as they realized a group of three individuals was extremely vulnerable to recapture. On the second occasion, an enemy patrol captured Balbir and Parab in north Burma. While being taken to the enemy camp, they managed to flee into the dense jungle. Captain Pritam Singh came to India via Tamu in Manipur. The other two escapees moved north through Myitkyina and came in contact with a patrol of Kachin Scouts in upper Burma. They were flown from Sumprabum (Burma) to Tinsukia (India).

All three officers later continued service with the Army of independent India and led glorious lives. Sadly, none of them is alive today, but their remarkable escapade has touched many lives and is often quoted as a great saga of grit and resolute determination.

In 1988, nearly half a century after the escape, Balbir retraced his footsteps along the route they had followed and met all those who had helped in their flight. He found that many of the brave-hearts who had so generously assisted them with money, shelter and sometimes vital information, had passed away. He, however, met and thanked their surviving children and relatives.

Especially touching was his meeting with the daughter of Khan Zaman, a Pathan cattle smuggler, who had lived with his

Thai wife at Prachu-ab-Khirikan, on the east coast of Thailand. Khan Zaman, who used to run a meat shop at Prachu, had helped the escapees proceed to Burma. Though both Khan Zaman and his Thai wife had passed away, their daughter, who had been a bubbly little toddler in May 1942, spent a long time chatting withBalbir.

She was very relieved to see him and told him that soon after their departure, a Japanese patrol had come toPrachu-ab-Khirikan with some Thai policemen. The Japanese had gathered the inhabitants together and announced that the three Allied escapees had been recaptured and shot dead. They had warned the people of dire consequences if they ever helped any prisoners who had escaped from Japanese custody. The lady added that the Japanese announcement had greatly saddened both her parents, who would often talk about the three escapees and their courageous flight and long journey from Singapore.

I could learn only a few details of the entire episode during my father's lifetime, as he rarely spoke about their great adventure. However, he wrote a couple of articles about it in the Journal of Kumaon Regiment. I managed to piece together the incredible story after listening with rapt attention to my father's rare descriptions of the escape and by reading his articles.

Colonel GS Parab also wrote a short account of the escape. When I discussed the exciting article penned by Colonel GS Parab with my father, he remembered and recounted a few more interesting details of their journey to India.

In 1976, a few years after being commissioned in 4 Kumaon, I undertook a trip to Singapore, Malaysia and Thailand and generally travelled along the route that was followed by the escapees. During my travels, I obtained valuable details and managed to get a closer feel of the great adventure.

I sincerely thank Colonel Narendra Singh, Commanding Officer of 4 Kumaon (1978 to 1981), for obtaining a copy of the escapees' interrogation report—*Interrogation Report [CSDIC (India), Red Fort, Delhi, (No 2 Section Report No 16, dated 2 November, 1942)]*—from London, UK, in 2007. The report contains a wealth of historical data and information about the escape, and I have used it liberally in my writing.

The book's second part is about Pritam's exploits in Kashmir, his heroic defence of Poonch, and the fateful sequence of events leading to his tragic court-martial.

I am very grateful to Lieutenant General Harwant Singh, Major General RK Khanna, Major General RS Mehta, Shiv Kunal Verma and other enlightened scholars for the meticulous and detailed research they have done to recount the latter part of Pritam's life. Their comprehensive studies have dramatically helped me in the writing of this book. I sincerely thank them for their great efforts.

Finally, I dedicate this book to the memory of Brigadier Pritam Singh, MC—one of the finest soldiers of the Indian Army.

"Valley View Villa" November 2019
Village Naini, P.O. Kalika,
Ranikhet 263645 (Uttarakhand)

Postscript

Serendipity played its role before the completion of this book. Just as we were giving finishing touches to the manuscript for printing and publishing, my co-author Pankaj P Singh chanced upon the two-volume autobiography of Major General DK Palit, VrC—*Musings & Memories.* Monty Palit, as a young and inexperienced Lieutenant Colonel, was the Commanding Officer of 3/9 GR when it was flown into Poonch during January-February 1948 to become part of the Poonch Garrison under Pritam's command.

Palit participated in, and witnessed first-hand, the action there and recorded a blow-by-blow account in his memoirs. It was a statement of his that was used to press the most serious charge—that of murder—against Pritam during the latter's court-martial.

The facts that emerge from Palit's account are shocking and trigger disbelief at the magnitude of the injustice meted out to Pritam. Many decades later, in his published memoirs, Palit says, "I decided that even at this late stage I should try to do something 'to restore justice to his (Pritam's) memory'—if not to annul the court-martial's verdict and sentence, at least to alleviate the character-damage done to him and, if possible, obtain a posthumous pardon from the President of India."

Writing on, he says, "... if there is any formal move to re-open Pritam's case and grant him a posthumous acquittal and exoneration, my statement would clearly help in the process. I have, therefore, decided to record my story and to send it to you (to the then Director USI) for use in whatever way that might promote Pritam's cause ... I have served under senior Indian Generals in the field and in peace. No one ever measured up to the immaculate and dauntless leadership of Pritam Singh. What can one do, nearly fifty years after the event, to restore justice to his memory?"

Having discovered the one testimony that lays bare the unpalatable truth, we have now added a chapter before our appeal, which reproduces as an excerpt all that Monty Palit had to say of his former Brigade Commander Pritam Singh. That, and this:

> Each time a man stands up for an ideal, or acts to improve the lot of others, or strikes out against injustice, he sends forth a tiny ripple of hope, and crossing each other from a million different centers of energy and daring those ripples build a current which can sweep down the mightiest walls of oppression and resistance.
>
> —*Robert F Kennedy*

Introduction

> One of the mainstays of an army is its esprit de corps, that spirit which gives a soldier purpose and the endurance to carry on where others might give up.
>
> —*Anonymous*

Pritam belonged to a noble family of Village Dina in Ferozepur, Punjab. After the battles of Chamkaur Sahib and Muktsar, Guru Gobind Singh, the last Sikh Guru, had stayed for some time in Dina. Here he wrote the famous epistle *Zafarnama* to the Mughal Emperor Aurangzeb. Pritam grew up there, and as a young man, attained a strong, soldierly bearing, with an impressive height of over six feet. Keen on joining the military, he gained a commission in the British-Indian Army and joined 4/19 Hyderabad Regiment (present 4 Kumaon) at Secunderabad in 1938.

The 4/19 Hyderabad Regiment (4 Kumaon) has had a remarkable history ever since Nawab Salabat Khan raised it in 1788 at Ellichpore (now Achalpur, Maharashtra). The unit established an enviable record of operational service beginning in Central India, then in China in 1900–1901, East Africa in 1914–1915, Afghanistan in 1919 and Iraq in 1923–1924. Before it moved to Secunderabad from Quetta (now in Pakistan) in 1936, it was involved in significant relief operations following the massive earthquake that struck the area on the night of 31 May 1935. The quake had caused untold damage and destruction, and for its stellar role during the relief operations, the unit received a Citation of Merit from Lord Willingdon, then Viceroy of India. Besides, Lance Naik Mata Din was awarded the coveted George Cross for gallantly risking his life to rescue two civilians buried deep in the rubble.

Happy days at Secunderabad (1937-39)

Presentation of Colours on 4 Dec 1937

At Secunderabad, the unit was a part of the local garrison, and a company was deployed at Bolarum. It participated in numerous military duties and parades. Just before Pritam joined 4/19 Hyderabad Regiment, it was presented with Colours on 4 December 1937, by Lieutenant General JES Brind, KCB, KBE, CMG, DSO, GOC-in-C Southern Command, in a glittering military parade. The Colours were received by Indian officers (Captain K Bhagwati Singh and Lieutenant Dilsukh Maan) for the very first time.

Lieutenant Pritam Singh (standing, fourth from left) and others at the wedding of Captain Azam Khan, in Secunderabad (1938). Later, Azam became a Lieutenant General in the Pakistan Army and Governor of East Pakistan

With political situations worsening across the world, the unit received orders thrice to move to an undisclosed destination. On the first two occasions, the orders for the move were cancelled. Finally, in August 1939, the unit landed in Madras (now Chennai) by rail under Lieutenant Colonel D Stuart, OBE with orders to sail on the ten-thousand-ton ship, the SS *Tilawa*. It sailed as part of the 12 Indian Infantry Brigade [Force "EMU"]. The Brigade Commander was Brigadier Paris, and other infantry battalions of the brigade were 2nd Battalion, Argyll & Sutherland Highlanders (A&SH) and 5/2 Punjab Regiment. In those days, sealed orders bearing the units' destination were ceremonially opened only once the ship was sailing on the high seas. In this case, Stewart opened the orders on the high seas out of Madras harbour, and amidst great excitement, he officially declared that the unit was proceeding to Singapore.

Officers and VCOs of 4/19 Hyderabad Regiment before leaving for Singapore in August 1939 (Lieutenant Pritam Singh is standing in middle row, fifth from right)

4/19 Hyderabad Regiment moving from Madras to Singapore aboard the SS Tilawa in August 1939

Lieutenant Pritam Singh in 4/19 Hyderabad Regiment

Singapore and Malaya

> I just love the Corps. I love the brotherhood, the camaraderie. I thank anyone in uniform who serves their fellow man. I love this country for so many reasons. We have such a great country here, and it's worth defending, and it's worth sacrificing for.
>
> —*Rob Riggle, US Marine Lieutenant Colonel*

On arrival, the unit stayed for a few days on a small island named Pulao Blakang Matti, located just off the coast of Singapore. After that, the accommodation shifted to tents pitched on the grounds of Tanglin in Singapore island, till the construction of wooden hutments at Tyersall Park there was complete. The 2nd Battalion, Manchester Regiment, already occupied some of the new hutments at Tyersall Park, and they later moved to north Singapore. The location of the wooden hutments was near the Botanical Garden in the estate of the Sultan of Johore.

In addition to 4/19 Hyderabad Regiment, Tyersall Park also housed HQ 12 Indian Infantry Brigade, A&SH and 12 Indian

General Hospital. The third infantry unit (5/2 Punjab) got located adjacent to the Singapore Naval Base, some 15 miles to the north of Singapore City.

Captain SM Shrinagesh (later General and Governor) was the Adjutant, and Captain Azam Khan (later Lieutenant General and Governor of East Pakistan) was the Quartermaster (QM). Shrinagesh got posted to India in December 1939, and he handed over his duties of Adjutant to Captain MG Jilani (later Major General and Adjutant General of the Pakistan Army). Major KS Thimayya (later General) was one of the company commanders. He, too, was posted back to India from Singapore.

With the outbreak of World War II, units were raised rapidly in India for deployment in the Middle-East sector (Egypt). Older ones like 4/19 Hyderabad Regiment were asked to repatriate some experienced troops for these new raisings, which then fought with distinction in Egypt, suffering heavy casualties.

In Singapore, the seasoned personnel sent to the new formations were replaced with raw recruits and reservists from 19th Hyderabad Regiment Training Centre at Agra and other training centres. The raw replacements adversely affected the battle-worthiness of the units, and considerable time and effort was expended in imparting basic training to the freshly arrived soldiers.

Besides their lack of training, the personnel arrived in Singapore without rifles, steel helmets and other essential battle equipment. So much so that some ignorant staff officer in India had even ordered them to move to Singapore with only chaguls—small, canvas water carriers! The overall state of the unit's equipment, too, was disappointing. More than half the rifles were of pre-1918 vintage. The weapons had been in use in East Africa and Persia during World War I—more than a quarter of a century earlier!

Malaya (now called Malaysia) was at that time a British colony on the mainland to the north of Singapore. It consisted of several states that were ruled by Sultans. The people were a mix of numerous races. A majority of the population consisted of indigenous Malays. However, there were some Europeans, Indians (mainly Tamils and Sikhs) and Chinese.

Singapore was even then a modern, cosmopolitan city, and it compared favourably with larger cities of the world. Life in Singapore was enjoyable when the battalion arrived from India. There were good hotels and a lot of social activity. People of Indian descent were particularly happy to see units with Indian troops. The troops could spend time in numerous bazaars and bathe in the sea on clean beaches. Some officers bought cars and toured around Malaya, while others visited the historical temples at Angkor Wat, in Cambodia (now Kampuchea).

It was a popular affair for officers to visit the Sea View Hotel on Sunday mornings and play a game of badminton or tennis. Later, they would have breakfast while watching huge breakers come crashing onto the shore. After the fall of France, the atmosphere there would often be surcharged with emotion. The men and women would stand up and sing in chorus the well-known wartime song of those days: "There will always be England; and England shall be free ..." Tears used to well up in the eyes of many a young woman in the gathering!

The mainland of Malaya had thick jungles where jungle-warfare training was held. The island of Singapore too had some dense jungles that provided equally good training facilities without going to Malaya. Thailand, in those days, had a poorly demarcated border with Malaya that ran alongside the thick jungles and low hills.

Topographically, the Malayan peninsula has a spine of hilly terrain with lush jungles and relatively flat coastal plains on both sides that are intersected by numerous rivers. Its climate is tropical with heavy rainfall around the year. Swampy areas near the rivers at that time, choked with dense undergrowth, vines and creepers, made movement difficult. Large areas were also under rubber plantations, and the rubber trees added to problems of poor visibility in the jungle. Movement across the country was strenuous too, except along fields of paddy cultivation and pineapple plantations. Overall, the terrain was difficult for operations and posed immense logistics problems. It was, however, ideally suited for infiltration, ambush and sneak attacks.

Lieutenant Colonel Stuart, CO of 4/19 Hyderabad Regiment, ensured that his unit trained for jungle-warfare at various locations on the Malayan peninsula. There was much to learn, and officers made sure that the troops gained the confidence to operate independently among the trees and dense undergrowth. They learned to move silently in primary jungles. However, in the secondary jungle, a path had to be cut to allow for any movement. This hacking of undergrowth invariably made a lot of noise, and the progress of troops was plodding. At some places, the jungle was so dense, that it took a whole day for troops to cut a track through the undergrowth and advance a mere 10 km!

It became an established procedure to arrange the men in "buddy pairs". Usually, friends were put together in such a way that they looked after one another. That ensured that the troops did not become separated from the rest nor got lost, and were able to provide help to one another when needed. Following this method avoided many unnecessary casualties when the unit went into action. In the jungle, a few steps taken unknowingly in the wrong direction could make one lose contact with his companions, and it was impossible to regain contact for hours! When a man had his neighbour tasked to look after him, he was less likely to get lost after that, and he confidently knew that help was always at hand.

During jungle training, troops were horrified when for the first time they found themselves covered with leeches. But they soon learned to remove the leeches by touching them with the lighted end of a *bidi*, cigarette or by merely sprinkling some edible salt on them. Survival in the jungle was an essential aspect of the unit's training and obtaining drinking water was one of the biggest problems faced by troops. So troops were taught how they could always find freshwater by cutting lianas or the one-inch thick creeper vines that festooned the trees everywhere in the jungle. The water which dripped out from the severed end of lianas was clear, cold and did not have an unpleasant taste. The jungle was teeming with wild animals of various kinds that were quite friendly unless attacked. Normally, they kept out of the way of the troops.

Monkeys frequently followed the soldiers and chattered shrilly as they moved about, high in the trees. The troops learnt happily that the monkeys would give a shrill warning of any approaching predators or humans. This warning was most invaluable during operations in the jungle because it allowed them to take cover before they were surprised by the sudden and untimely arrival of any enemy. Many types of snakes were encountered during the jungle training as well, and the men could not easily overcome their loathing towards the creepy and crawly reptiles. Rampant mosquitoes were a big problem in the jungle, and their painful bites often brought on frenzied itching and even a bout of dreaded malaria fever. Troops were issued small bottles containing a particular type of oil with a strong smell that was very useful in warding off the obnoxiousflying pests.

Singapore island lies on the southern tip of the Malayan peninsula and was (and still is) linked to the mainland with a strong concrete causeway. The island was the bastion of British power in the Far East, and the British converted it into a virtual fortress after spending over 60 million pounds on its defences.

There were sufficient stocks of ammunition, rations and water to sustain operations for at least six months. The island was also strongly guarded by its coastal batteries which covered the sea against naval landings.

Lieutenant Pritam Singh, in the meanwhile, had received posting orders to proceed to 3/16 Punjab Regiment, also located in Singapore at that time. The new unit was quite a change from 4/19 Hyderabad Regiment as it had a different class composition of troops comprising Punjabi Muslims, Sikhs and Dogras. The regimental badge consisted of a Maltese Cross with a Muslim Crescent and a Sikh Quoit, surmounted by a Tudor crown with a scroll of the Regiment's name. The Training Battalion of 16 Punjab Regiment was located at Multan in Punjab. Pritam often met his old colleagues from 4/19 Hyderabad Regiment and exchanged notes.

Crest of 16 Punjab Regiment

During 1940 and 1941, the Allies had imposed a trade embargo on Japan, and intelligence gathered by them indicated a Japanese plan for taking Singapore. The British felt that a Japanese advance through the thick jungles of Malaya was not a viable proposition due to difficult terrain and extended lines of communication (more than 700 miles)! Instead, they expected that Singapore would be attacked from the seaward side, an eventuality for which the island fortress was well prepared. On 8 December 1941, the Japanese 25th Army invaded northern Malaya and Thailand, attacking Pearl Harbour at almost the same time and sucking the United States into the war.

Although there were some airfields in northern Malaya, the theatre was woefully short of aircraft. Also, British experts had categorically stated that tanks were of no use in close country, so no Allied tanks were inducted! While the Infantry Divisions held a few anti-tank mines, ironically, these mines were kept in reserve, and the units were hardly issued any of these!

When operations did finally commence, the mines could neither stop nor deter the Japanese tanks. Infantry battalions were given a few lightly armoured carriers, which were tracked vehicles with an LMG mounted on the open top and equipped with a limited number of Bouys anti-tank rifles. Some vintage Lancaster armoured cars were also available, and later these were replaced by the more modern Mormon-Harrington armoured cars. However, none of the anti-tank equipment was a match for Japanese tanks that supported their lightning offensive.

These shortfalls were to have severe repercussions on the conduct of defensive operations, and they would prove to be the most prominent factors responsible for the Allied defeat in Malaya.

It had been appreciated earlier that in the less likely eventuality of a land-based offensive, Japanese landings could take place at Singora and Pattani beaches in Thailand. Thus, detailed reconnaissance had been carried out and a plan—*Operation Matador*—put in place to immediately send troops to cover both the beaches.

As events unfolded, Japanese landings took place at these very beaches. However, the plan to send forces to contest the Japanese landings was inexplicably never implemented. They were initially resisted by a few Thai Army units, while the Allied formations in north Malaya waited at the Malaya-Thailand border to see what would happen!

The British strength in Malaya consisted of 9 and 11 Indian Infantry Divisions of 3 Indian Corps under Lieutenant General Percival. Both these divisions had only two brigades each. The remaining two brigade groups were earmarked as reserves for 3 Indian Corps.

Soon, both units—3/16 Punjab Regiment and 4/19 Hyderabad Regiment—proceeded north to Malaya to stop the rapidly advancing Japanese forces.

They fought bitter actions and suffered heavy casualties in the process. These actions were young Pritam's first experience of combat operations, and he performed creditably in the difficult jungle battles. The two units of 16 Punjab Regiment fell back under enormous pressure, and they both suffered hefty casualties. They were captured after the Battle of Singapore and interned in Bidadari POW Camp.

Prisoners in Nee Soon

The two most powerful warriors are patience and time.

—*Leo Tolstoy*

On 13 February 1942, heavy Japanese bombardment and air attacks were taking place on Fortress Singapore. The end came rather quickly at 7 PM on 14 February 1942, when Singapore City fell to the Japanese, and after that, only random small arms firing could be heard. Lieutenant General AE Percival signed an unconditional surrender on the very next day. Together with the Singapore garrison of 70,000 men, the remnants of 4/19 Hyderabad Regiment, 3/16 Punjab Regiment and other units, became prisoners-of-war (POWs).

Just before the fall, units had been asked to submit names of officers who were not in actual command of troops and who possessed expertise in jungle warfare. Such officers were to be sent back to India to train soldiers for the raising of new units and formations. Major (later Lieutenant General) K Bahadur

Singh of 4/19 Hyderabad Regiment was one of those selected to proceed to India. He was given letters by his officers that were to be stamped and posted in India. Unfortunately, the Japanese torpedoed the ship carrying this party and sunk it, killing many of the personnel on board. Many others were captured and sent back to Singapore, and Major K Bahadur Singh was amongst those who re-joined his unit in the POW camp there. He was later responsible for devotedly looking after the battalion in the camp.

Major K Bahadur Singh

During the Battle of Singapore, a devastating Japanese air raid took place on the city and bombs struck the location of 3/16 Punjab Regiment. Captain Pritam Singh was among those seriously wounded during this air raid. Some of his troops lifted him, placed him on a stretcher, and carried him to a nearby military hospital. Pritam received proper care from the dedicated medical staff there and recovered. He was thereafter sent to the Bidadari POW Camp where his unit—3/16 Punjab Regiment—was interned.

Japanese troops march through Singapore on 17 Feb 1942

On 17 February, the Japanese authorities ordered the collection of all weapons. European prisoners were taken to the Changi POW Camp, whereas Asian officers and troops were marched to Farrar Park, where they were paraded in front of a large pavilion. The officers and men were allowed to take only the clothing they wore and carry two rations of food. On the arrival of a Major Fujiwara (from Japanese Intelligence), Captain Konishita (a Japanese interpreter), Colonel Hunt (OC 2nd Echlon), Colonel Niranjan Singh Gill (INA), Captain Mohan Singh (INA) and Giani Pritam Singh at Farrar Park, all prisoners were ordered to stand up.

Col Niranjan Singh Gill

A brief aside on the two INA—Indian National Army—officers present that day, of whom Gill's role would later prove to be pivotal in the escape saga. The INA was a military wing formed with the help of the Japanese forces, and it fought alongside them against the British and Allied forces. At its peak, it comprised over 45,000 Indian POWs captured after the fall of Singapore. Mohan Singh headed it till April 1942. By then he developed differences with other INA leaders and the mantle passed on to Subhas Bose in 1943. Gill had studied at RIMC (Rashtriya Indian Military College), Dehradun and trained at RMA, Sandhurst, UK. He was among the first lot of Indian officers to join 4/19 Hyderabad Regiment and then served in the 19th Hyderabad Regiment Training Centre, Banares, in 1936. In 1936–37, he was again among the first Indian officers to be posted to Army HQ, New Delhi, when only British officers were posted there. After completing the Staff College course at Quetta, he proceeded to Malaya on a staff appointment. After the fall of Malaya and Singapore, Gill joined Indian National Army (INA) as a founder member with Mohan Singh, Shah Nawaz Khan and Gurdial Singh. After the War, he was tried by the British along with other senior officers of INA at Red Fort, Delhi. Still later, he served as India's ambassador to Panama in 1963–1964.

Back at Farrar Park, a brief ceremony took place. Colonel Hunt marched up to Major Fujiwara and said in English, "I hand over all Indian prisoners of war to the Japanese government". He proceeded to hand over some papers to the Major, turned around smartly and left. Fujiwara, in turn, handed the prisoners over to Captain Mohan Singh. Soon after, there were announcements over the loudspeakers in both English and Hindustani, asking the prisoners to be seated. They were then addressed successively by Major Fujiwara, Captain Mohan Singh and Giani Pritam Singh.

When the speeches were over, officers above the rank of Lieutenant were invited inside the pavilion and offered a drink of neat Australian brandy. During drinks, Major Fujiwara welcomed any officer who wanted to discuss any matter with him to step forward. The ceremony concluded after this, and officers of 4/19 Hyderabad Regiment were told to proceed to the Nee Soon POW Camp. Troops of the unit had already moved there earlier along with personnel of some other units.

The Nee Soon POW Camp was located towards the northern end of the island and comprised a series of ageing barracks built around a soccer ground. Though the camp could house about a thousand men, it ended up holding over twenty-two thousand prisoners! Over the next couple of days, the POW officers were addressed several times by both Captain Mohan Singh and Fujiwara. Mohan Singh's designation was General Officer Commanding (GOC), Indian National Army (INA) and Second Lieutenant Rattan Singh was his ADC. The GOC's staff comprised of personnel who were all promoted to the rank of officer. Mohan Singh urged that every officer was welcome to see him anytime and have frank discussions with him on any issue. His HQ was in the Police Barracks, between Thompson Road and Bukit Timah Road.

The Administrative Committee of the Nee Soon Camp comprised of seven Indian officers, including Colonel Gill of the INA and Captain Munnawar Hussein of 4/19 Hyderabad Regiment, who served as his assistant. The others were Major Kiani (14 Punjab Regiment), Colonel Gilani (Indian State Force [Bahawalpur]), Colonel Chatterjee (Indian Medical Service), Captain Kashyap (15 Field Company Madras Sappers & Miners), and Lieutenant Colonel Bhonsale (Garhwal Rifles).

These officers lived adjacent to the Nee Soon POW Camp. The functions of the Committee members were purely administrative, and they did not carry out any propaganda on the prisoners. The members functioned through Captain Mohan Singh, who was in general control with the Japanese. Only Mohan Singh, M. Akram and the Japanese officers attempted propaganda on the prisoners of war. The Head of Administrative Committee was Major Shah Nawaz Khan of 14 Punjab Regiment.

Colonel NS Gill was particularly active in improving the prisoners' conditions. He wielded high authority and on many occasions, obtained immediate results by his interventions. Often while lecturing the officers on the necessity of discipline, saluting and living with honour and dignity as prisoners of war, he endeavoured in every way to keep up the morale of the prisoners. At no time did Gill or any of the other Administrative Committee members try to persuade Indian prisoners to either go over to the Japanese or join the INA. The INA did not exist in any of the camps where the Indian prisoners were interned. In Singapore, the INA had a separate camp called Volunteer's Camp, which consisted mainly of Indian Army personnel captured during fighting on the mainland of Malaya. In Singapore, there were seven POW Camps in which Indian Army personnel were interned.

Most Indian personnel had been shocked at the sudden turn of events that had led to their humiliating status as prisoners. They felt let down, particularly since most of the Indian battalions had fought gallantly and suffered heavy casualties during the campaign in Malaya. They knew that the Japanese had also incurred heavy losses, and quite suddenly become their captors. Despite the overwhelming odds it had faced during battles in Malaya, Pritam's erstwhile unit, 4/19 Hyderabad Regiment, had gallantly carved a name for itself during the operations and won two battle honours—North Malaya and Slim River.

Apart from the Nee Soon Camp, there were six other POW Camps in Singapore for Indian Army personnel—Seletar,

Bidadari (Alkaff Gardens), Tyersall Park, Buller, Tengah Aerodrome (Fatigue Camp) and Kranji Camp. The heads of the Administrative Committees of Seletar and Bidadari camps were Lieutenant Colonel Ushaq (1 Hyderabad Infantry) and Lieutenant Colonel Nagar (RIASC) respectively. Lieutenant Colonel Gurbux Singh (Jind Forces) headed Tyresall Park camp while Captain Pharnavis (4/19 Hyderabad Regiment) headed the Buller camp. He later took charge of BT Camp. Major Ghanshyam Singh (RIASC) was the head at Fatigue camp, while the head of the Kranji camp Administrative Committee is not known.

Overcrowded conditions in Nee Soon POW Camp were unbearable. However, the unit hierarchy and functioning of the command system were kept intact. Troops were accommodated in ramshackle barracks and cared for by section and platoon appointment holders. Medicines were scarce and flies abounded in their thousands. The congested living conditions added to the men's misery. Water arrangements were terrible, and twenty to thirty men died of dysentery in the first month of captivity. The heat, humidity and working conditions added to the men's thirst. Water was scarce and unclean. It was barely enough for the men to quench their thirst. After the first month, conditions improved somewhat, and the water supply got better. But, overall health care continued to be pathetic. The camp had a small hospital, where about four hundred patients were admitted at all times, mostly suffering from dysentery. Due to congested living conditions and free breeding of mosquitoes, diseases like dysentery and malaria were rampant.

Flies bred in thousands in the camp and men were dying every day. Doctors among the prisoners did their very best with limited stocks of medicines. They provided succour and saved the lives of many men. Although all POW doctors worked in the hospital, there was still a shortage of medical staff and medicines. All civil hospitals in Singapore had been taken over by the Japanese for their sick and wounded soldiers. Allied casualties were moved out of these hospitals and sent to POW Camps. Many died there because of lack of care and medicines.

In addition to the pathetic conditions in the camp, the behaviour of Japanese guards was rude and offensive. They had an indifferent attitude and were rather uncouth in their behaviour. At the slightest pretext, they brutally beat the prisoners and employed various forms of demeaning physical punishments. Severe torture of prisoners was common, and some were even bayoneted to death or beheaded for flimsy reasons. Prisoners were supposed to salute all Japanese and INA personnel. Japanese guards often made it a point to strut before officer and VCO prisoners, either in the camp or during fatigue duties. If they did not receive a smart salute, they would physically assault the unfortunate officer or VCO. Twice, some VCOs of 11 Infantry Division Transport Company were beaten badly during fatigues and had to be hospitalised with severe injuries. When reported to the senior Japanese officer present, he said that beatings were necessary to maintain discipline and were the norm in the Japanese Army. He added that the physical punishments need not unduly perturb the prisoners.

There were shortages of food in all Japanese occupied territories, especially sugar, flour, milk and oil. In Nee Soon Camp, unit cooks prepared food for the prisoners in dark and dingy enclosures called *langar.* The cooks used provisions received from either the administrative staff or from the Japanese. At first, wheat flour was available to make *rotis.* After that, only rice was provided to the cooks, resulting in a watery, rice gruel. Rations were limited, and there were no arrangements for the supply of fresh vegetables or lentils. On some special days, the prisoners were delighted to see a few vegetable leaves added to the swill. Sometimes, boiled rice was served with watery lentils or *dal.* It was said that the European prisoners in Changi POW Camp sometimes received tinned fish or meat, but their diet too comprised mainly of boiled rice. Rarely, the men received cigarettes, tea leaves, sugar and salt, but no milk.

Every morning at dawn, the prisoners were ordered to assemble at different locations in the camp. The unit had to fall-in daily in a large playing field, at the centre of the camp. Here, the men were physically counted, and a report was given to the Japanese officer or senior Japanese NCO present.

Japanese atrocities

Although some personnel were weak with dysentery or malaria, they had to be present in the assembly, and get included in the count before the Japanese officer/senior NCO. Only personnel admitted in the hospital were allowed to be absent from the morning fall-in. It was heart-rending to see some of the sick personnel fall to the ground with exhaustion. They lay there writhing in pain for half-an-hour or so till all prisoners dispersed for their work details. No one was permitted to break ranks and help those unfortunate men who had collapsed during the fall-in. Hours of work were from 6.30 AM to 10 AM and again from 12 Noon to 5 PM. Japanese sentries would tell the prisoners with pride that in Japan, they were used to starting work during early hours of the morning before the sun had risen.

The morale of prisoners from the fighting arms was generally good. However, some prisoners from the Labour Corps and other services had a deplorable march discipline and were an embarrassment to troops from the fighting arms. Regular troops were in good shape, especially the European prisoners, who could often be heard singing songs loudly as they marched for fatigue duties. For whatever reason, the Japanese frowned upon Indian and Australian officers talking to one another.

One day, an Australian column halted near a fatigue party from the Nee Soon Camp. Soon, the Japanese guards of both parties were engaged in an animated discussion. Finding an opportune moment, one of the Indian officers Captain Balbir Singh cautiously approached the column and asked a thin and ragged looking Australian prisoner about the conditions in their camp. The Australian soldier winked and replied with a half-smile, "Things could be worse, Mate. In any case, it is not for long—already the Americans have landed in Java". The reply summed up the positive attitude of the Australian prisoners in Singapore, although they were rather ill-informed about the Americans landing in Java. Balbir had been the Company Commander of "B" Company, 4/19 Hyderabad Regiment, before being taken POW.

A six-feet deep and six-feet wide trench had been dug around the Nee Soon POW Camp as a security obstacle to deter escape by the prisoners. Pairs of armed Japanese and INA sentries patrolled along the outer edge of the trench. The sentries were rude and gruff to any prisoner who tried to call out and make conversation with the Australian prisoners. Invariably, the Japanese guards made threatening gestures with their rifles and fixed bayonets.

On 11 March 1942, the Camp Commandant of Nee Soon Camp ordered 500 men of 4/19 Hyderabad Regiment to leave and proceed to a new camp near Bukit Panjang Village, under Captain Balbir Singh. Another fellow regimental officer of Balbir and survivor of the Japanese onslaught on 4/19 Hyderabad Regiment at Slim River, Captain Gangaram Parab, accompanied him. The camp was located at 9½ Milestone, on Bukit-Timah Road, about six miles from the new aerodrome being built at Tengah and was called Fatigue Camp. Prisoners were housed in old huts, which had been repaired by the troops on their arrival. Major Ghanshyam Singh was in-charge of the new Fatigue Camp, while Balbir was senior officer among prisoners of 4/19 Hyderabad Regiment.

Soon, the Japanese put all prisoners to work. Personnel of 4/19 Hyderabad Regiment were taken daily for construction work at Tengah Airfield. The prisoners worked on the construction of runways and airport buildings. The engineers were all Japanese while prisoners provided the labour force and did all the hard work. They were made to break stones and haul cement sacks and other material for the building work. The prisoners' lack of nourishment had a telling effect when they were made to toil for long hours in the hot sun. Indiscriminate floggings and humiliation by Japanese guards were routine happenings at the POW Camp. But, the threat of punishments did not dampen the spirits of the prisoners. They quietly told each other incredible stories and made plans for the wonderful time they would have when the war ended, and they got back to India and their homes.

A Japanese interpreter with a Japanese officer (Lieutenant Inova) used to visit the camp and oversee the work. On one occasion, a Japanese officer came to the camp to ascertain if work on the aerodrome could be hastened by increasing the number of men. A few days later, a platoon of Japanese Engineers arrived and erected a high wire-mesh fence around the camp. They also put a few searchlights on pillars. The lights were switched on daily at sunset, and their intense beams swept along the fence. This effort by the Japanese was aimed at preventing any prisoners from escaping from the camp at night. The Japanese Engineers worked for about a week and then departed. No help was sought from the prisoners, who continued with their work at Tengah Aerodrome.

Escape from Captivity

> If I am captured I will continue to resist by all means available. I will make every effort to escape and to aid others to escape.
>
> —*United States Military Code Of Conduct, Military Rules For Prisoners Of War, Article III*

Both Captain Balbir Singh and Captain Gangaram Parab had been planning to escape ever since they got captured. But things were chaotic, and indiscriminate shooting was often taking place. Also, as they were the only officers of 4/19 Hyderabad Regiment at the new camp, they felt their presence was essential for the welfare of the troops. Their escape was likely to be promptly discovered by the Japanese, leading to re-capture, brutal punishments and even death by bayonet thrusts or beheading.

Whenever they moved out for construction work at Tengah Airfield, the officers' reviewed their plans. They hoped to get a boat or *sampan* to make for any of the islands near Singapore and then somehow reach India. However, it was a dangerous plan, since the Japanese meticulously guarded the coast and harbour areas. Even if they managed to procure a boat, they had little knowledge of handling a craft in the open sea.

By mid-April of 1942, Major Pharnavis, Captain Dil Sukh Maan and Captain Ramaniah, the Regimental Medical Officer (RMO), with about 300 to 400 men from 4/19 Hyderabad Regiment, also moved to the Fatigue Camp, thus, making the escape easier. Captain Pritam Singh used to come over from the Bidadari camp with the assistance of Major GR Nagar, formerly of 4/19 Hyderabad Regiment. Nagar had joined the INA and was on the Administrative Committee of that camp.

On the prison grapevine, Pritam had heard of the escape plans hatched by his erstwhile colleagues Balbir and Parab. As he was eager to return to India, Pritam asked Balbir to include him in the proposed escape attempt. Balbir and Parab thought it over and agreed.

There was by now an acute shortage of accommodation and food on Singapore island. The Japanese decided to allow civilians to return to their homes on the mainland with permits issued by them. The three of them knew that their capture by the Japanese would mean brutal torture followed by almost certain death.

Thus, in preparation for their escape, they changed their names and posed as clerks from a rubber estate. While on fatigue duty to Singapore City, Balbir and Parab managed to enrol themselves as civilian members of the India Independence League (IIL) and obtained the necessary travel permits. They also obtained an IIL membership for Pritam. While Balbir assumed the identity of Bhajan Singh, a former clerk with the Censor Office, Parab became Prem Singh, a sports dealer. Pritam donned the mantle of Balwant Singh, also a former clerk in Censor Office.

Since the prisoners were becoming physically weaker with each passing day due to dysentery, malaria and other diseases, they decided to speed up the escape. They secretly smuggled clothes, rations and money into the camp. Although short of quinine and other drugs, Captain Ramaniah, the RMO, arranged some valuable medicines for the escape. In the meanwhile, Pritam got himself transferred to Nee Soon POW Camp through "friends" in the Bidadari Camp Administrative Committee.

Another POW, Lieutenant Balwant Singh, formerly of 4/19 Hyderabad and later 5/14 Punjab, often expressed his keen desire to join the trio in their escape bid.

Balbir, Parab and Pritam discussed the matter in detail. However, they felt that four escapees would be easily discovered and apprehended by the Japanese. It would be far too dangerous to include Balwant in the escape bid.

When they told Balwant that he could not join the escape bid, he was quiet. It seemed that he had a premonition of his fate—he was subsequently shipped to Borneo and bayoneted to death for a minor infringement of POW camp rules. Much later, his widow would chastise Balbir for not allowing Balwant to join in the escape to India.

Lieutenant Balwant Singh

Specific administrative arrangements were made by the three officers to facilitate their escape. Balbir procured some rough, off-white material from an old tent. He asked the unit tailor to stitch from it a baggy shirt and pyjama-type trousers with a draw-string made from a couple of shoelaces bound together. During the escape, he wore it along with a white *puggaree* and canvas PT shoes. He deliberately avoided khaki, which was a more military colour. With Pritam included in the escape, Balbir had similar clothes stitched for him from the remaining tent material. Parab bought a pair of off-white trousers and canvas PT shoes for one Straits Dollar each (the official currency introduced by the Japanese).

Parab found a civilian hat at the Royal Artillery barracks at the Nee Soon Camp. Though it looked rather outlandish, it was very convenient for concealing a portion of a map salvaged from a bungalow near the Bukit Panjang Village Camp. That little piece of map originally belonged to a school book and proved very valuable as it showed Malaya, Thailand, Burma and parts of eastern India. It helped them to plan the general route they would follow, and more importantly, it depicted the boundaries of the various countries that lay on the way. It also showed the different stretches of sea waters they might encounter during their journey to India.

Next, they urgently required money for tickets, travel expenses, permits, food and other expenses during the escape. It had to be borrowed mainly from traders in Singapore and some larger towns on the way. There was little or no money with the prisoners in both the Nee Soon and Fatigue camps. However, one enterprising VCO of 4/19 Hyderabad Regiment named Subedar Trilok Singh gave a surprise. He generously lent them a princely sum of Indian Rupees 60 which he had carefully hidden within a deep crack in the barracks wall at Fatigue Camp.

Some Indian traders in Singapore assisted them with more money and information. There was a well-known sports-gear shop on the North Bridge Road named Rose and

Company. Both Pritam and Balbir were friendly with a trader there named Labh Singh. He magnanimously loaned them 70 Straits Dollars.

After considerable discussion and paying some graft, Balbir ensured that the money was collected from Labh Singh through a friendly Malay watchman at the railway crossing near the Fatigue camp. The watchman was not aware of the soon-to-be-executed escape attempt and inadvertently told Pritam and Balbir that the sale of rail tickets to the public had recommenced from 1 May 1942. The Japanese wanted to enable the maximum number of civilians to proceed to mainland Malaya and ease the desperate food situation in Singapore island. Till then, only special military trains and goods trains were functioning from Singapore. Enterprising civilians used to travel surreptitiously on the goods trains. But getting on them was rather tricky, and there was always the danger of an accident.

Balbir and Company was another sports shop near Rose and Company. In peacetime, its proprietor Balkar Singh, an affable and friendly Sikh, frequently travelled between Bangkok and Malaya. He had some relatives in Bangkok who were in the cloth and garments trade. Balbir knew Balkar well, for as captain of the unit hockey team he used to purchase hockey equipment from the latter's shop.

During one of their rare visits to the Singapore market as members of a working party from the POW camp, the trio went to Balkar's shop and began talking to him. They spoke about the changing times after the Japanese invasion and other issues like hardships in the POW camps. Then, in confidence, they told him about their plans to escape to India via Malaya and Burma.

Completely supportive, Balkar too chipped in with a loan, and they now had at their disposal 210 Straits Dollars and 60 Indian Rupees. Balkar also passed on a photograph of a relative of his named Jaswant Singh. Jaswant was a former Captain in the Royal Dutch Army and settled on the island of Sumatra where there was a small Sikh community.

Captain Jaswant Singh, Royal Dutch Army

Interestingly, Balkar recommended that they should escape from Singapore and then make their way by boat to Sumatra. He even promised to give them a letter for Jaswant, who, he said, would surely assist them in moving on to Australia.

Balkar's suggestion provided Pritam, Balbir and Parab with another exciting option for the escape, and they gave it a lot of thought. Finally, they rejected it as they did not want to venture into an unknown territory that was in the opposite direction of their destination, India. Nevertheless, Balbir wrapped Jaswant's photograph in a small piece of polythene and kept it in his pocket. This photo would prove to be providential during their interrogation by the Japanese Military Police after their capture at Monywa (Burma).

During their time at the BT Road Fatigue Camp, Balbir and Parab kept in contact with the Nee Soon Camp by often making individual visits to lodge complaints of neglect against their RMO Captain Ramaniah. At heart, they were grateful to him for giving them valuable quinine tablets, water sterilizing tablets and some bandages for their journey.

A worrisome reason cropped up to hasten the escape. The prisoners were told that a company of 4/19 Hyderabad Regiment (with both Balbir and Parab) was soon to be shipped to the Andaman Islands. Although no date had been set for the move, it was expected to take place during that very month.

So when Colonel Niranjan Singh Gill visited the Nee Soon POW Camp, Balbir confidentially told him about their proposed escape, and requested him to have the company's move to Andaman islands cancelled. Gill was uncertain whether the Japanese plans could be changed, and he suggested that Balbir and others escape from the Andaman islands and travel by boat to India. However, Balbir insisted on cancellation of the planned move to Andaman islands as it would be difficult to the escape from there and travel across the Andaman Sea and the Bay of Bengal. They had no expertise to negotiate the seas, and a journey by boat would be most hazardous. Gill agreed with Balbir's views and said he would try his best to convince the Japanese authorities to change their plans.

Every day they waited expectantly for the cancellation of the move to Andaman islands. Ten days passed, and no word was received from Gill. Meanwhile, the company received orders to sail for Andaman islands the following day. That day, Balbir and Parab lined up with the troops with a heavy heart. Vehicles were loaded, and the men awaited their final orders to move to Singapore Harbour, to set sail to the Andaman islands. Both officers found their plans doomed to fail even before they attempted escape.

Just then, a Jeep careened into the POW Camp at high speed. Colonel Gill was half standing in the co-driver's seat. He waved his arms above his head and shouted joyfully, "Balbir, Balbir, the move has been cancelled. You are not to go to the Andaman islands." Gill's arrival was providential and once again, the plans to escape sprang to life. The officers were elated, and they happily ordered the men to unload the vehicles and move back to the huts in the POW Camp.

The Bukit-Timah Road Fatigue Camp was centrally located on Singapore Island. It was about nine-and-a-half miles away from Singapore City. Soon, construction work at Tengah Airfield intensified, and the prisoners were taken daily in trucks to a nearby quarry to break stones and load them in vehicles. The vehicles then proceeded to Tengah Aerodrome, where another group of prisoners unloaded the stones.

After cancellation of the move to the Andaman islands, feverish preparations began for the escape to India. In consultation with other officers in the POW Camp, the date for escape was set for 4 May 1942.

Maj Pharnavis, the senior officer, promised to give Balbir, Parab and Pritam a clear head-start by concealing the escape from the Japanese for the first 24 hours. As part of the final preparations for the escape, a hole was surreptitiously cut in the camp's perimeter wire-fence and concealed with boulders, some burlap sacking and cut bushes.

The three officers were excited as they wore the clothes they had prepared for the escape. The clothes were meant to disguise the escapees, and make them look like Indian refugees who were moving out of Singapore, because of the latest Japanese orders. They would also carry small bundles containing a sheet, blanket, towel and some small personal items.

Before dusk on 4 May 1942, the three escaping officers were given a hearty meal prepared from carefully smuggled food supplies. A heart-rending parting took place with old comrades, including the JCOs and men.

After the touching farewell, the three officers left the barracks and silently moved close to the fence. They were aware that after dark, all movement outside the barracks was forbidden and could invite severe punishment, even death by being bayoneted or beheaded.

Once they neared the fence, they crouched down and waited in a fold in the ground. After confirming that there were no Japanese or INA guards around, Balbir sprinted forward and quickly slipped through the concealed hole in the fence. Once across, he lay prone and unmoving. He could hear his heart beat loudly with fear and excitement.

After confirming that he had not been seen, he signalled to the others with a raised hand, indicating that there were no enemy sentries in sight. Parab crawled through the hole in the fence, to be followed by Pritam.

Their great adventure had finally begun.

Balbir runs forward to get through the fence, while Parab and Pritam remain hidden in the undergrowth

Crossing into Thailand

It is not the mountain we conquer but ourselves.

—Edmund Hillary, O Magazine, April 2007

Once all three officers were across the fence, they rose to their feet and proceeded to the nearby Bukit-Timah Road. The trio walked alongside it for nearly ten miles before reaching their destination at the Singapore Railway Station. They made sure that they avoided lights and enemy guards. Luckily, due to Japanese restrictions, no vehicles were plying on the road at that late hour. Carefully, they began walking on the grass strip lining the sides of the road and proceeded towards Singapore City. It was a long walk, and the escapees gained confidence as they silently trudged along the dark and deserted side-streets of Singapore. They were glad to be finally on their way, having overcome the first hurdle of escaping from the POW camp.

At North Bridge Road, they came across a tram line that led to a tram station. Though it was not a part of their plan, building up courage, the trio went to the deserted tram station.

Soon, a well-lit tram rumbled noisily into the station, hooted its loud horn and ground to a halt. Silently, they boarded the tram and sat on well-worn and yellowing wooden seats. The only other passenger was an old and bedraggled Malay man, who was seated near the entrance and was looking out of the window. The conductor, a middle-aged Chinese man wearing a blue cotton coat, shuffled up to them with his leather bag. Since they had earlier travelled in Singapore trams before the Japanese occupation, they knew the procedure for sitting down and then buying their tickets. Balbir confidently bought three tickets to the Singapore Railway Station. The trio sat down to enjoy their newly found freedom. The streets were dark and deserted, and familiar shop signs flashed past the window as the tram swayed incessantly and clattered on its way. They got off at the Railway Station halt. The tram station was well lit, and several armed Japanese soldiers could be seen moving about in small groups.

After alighting, the trio waited for a while in the dark shadows near the tram-line. Finally, they mustered courage and walked confidently into Singapore Railway Station. Parab and Pritam were visibly uncomfortable when they had to sit on a bench directly below a bright electric light. Some Japanese soldiers appeared to be living on the platform, but no INA guards were seen. An armed Japanese soldier was pacing about on the platform. He periodically sauntered to the booking office before turning back the way he had come. A large number of Malays, with a sprinkling of some Sikhs and Tamils, were waiting on the platform to board the train. However, no one paid any attention to the three officers. Balbir stood behind the bench for a while and then walked briskly across to the ticket counter. He went forward only once the armed Japanese guard had turned his back and was moving the other way. Balbir easily negotiated for three train tickets to Prai, with the help of the IIL Cards. The tickets for Prai cost 10 Straits Dollars each. As he was paying for them, the sleepy Malay ticket clerk wanted to know where were the other two persons who would be travelling to Prai. Balbir was initially taken aback by the question, but he calmly satisfied the clerk by pointing to the bench where Parab and Pritam were sitting under the light. The clerk was speaking in Malay and had looked surprised to hear good, cultured English spoken by an individual wearing such nondescript clothes! However, without any further questions, the clerk had prepared three tickets and handed them to Balbir, who heaved a sigh of relief and joined the other two escapees. The clerk then busied himself with examining the money and counting it in repeatedly.

Having purchased the tickets, the trio felt more confident and spent the remainder of the night sitting on the wooden bench. Attention was avoided by sitting in one place and conversing only in low whispers. They deliberately avoided the numerous detachments of Japanese soldiers, and in the morning they boarded the train and sat well apart to avoid detection. Pritam sat next to a burly Sikh who was travelling to Alor Setar. A wood-burning steam-engine hauled the train over the repaired Singapore Causeway and through the densely forested and picturesque countryside of Malaya.

For the next day and night, the escapees sat quietly in the swaying, railway compartment, relieved that their great journey that had finally begun. The joy of successfully escaping from Singapore blocked out fears of recapture and anxieties of the torturous journeys that lay ahead. The rhythmic sounds of the train's wheels induced a deep slumber and very soon the three officers were dozing fitfully in the swaying compartment.

During the journey, they were not molested in any way. Only the ticket inspectors came among the passengers. As the names of railway stations flashed by, the three officers thought of the bitter battles they had fought not so long ago. Looking back at the turbulent days of fighting the Japanese, they considered themselves lucky to be alive and remembered the many gallant soldiers who lay forever in the deep jungles. Sadly, these brave soldiers would never return to their homes in faraway India. On many railway stations, they saw parties of armed Japanese soldiers who were billeted there while some soldiers stood like sentries, with rifles slung on their shoulders.

On the afternoon of 6 May, the train pulled into Prai. Here, Balbir got off and bought onward tickets for Alor Setar, by the same train. At about 7 PM on 6 May, the train steamed into Alor Setar, which was near the border with Thailand. While sitting in the railway compartment, Pritam had got into a conversation with a Sikh traveller named Dogar Singh, and had asked him if there was a Gurudwara in Alor Setar. Dogar Singh replied in the affirmative and offered to escort them there, but the three officers decided not to go along with him. During his conversation, Pritam had discovered that Dogar Singh was a PWD engineer who had earlier been removed from his job by the British for some misdeeds he had committed. The Japanese had now reinstated him. So Pritam never told Dogar Singh about their escape, and his background dissuaded the officers from using the Gurudwara for fears of recapture by the Japanese.

Thus, at the railway station the escapees quickly picked up their ragged bundles and alighted from the train. Without talking to anyone or asking for directions, they headed out of the township in the dark. Soon they were safely hidden in the jungles that surrounded Alor Setar.

To their great disappointment, the escapees discovered that to be able to cross the border from Malay into Thailand they would need valid passports stamped with endorsements by the Japanese occupation authorities. They decided to risk an attempt to cross over, and a few nights later the three moved through the jungle and approached a border crossing. Hidden in the undergrowth, they surveilled the spot. They saw it was guarded by an armed Japanese patrol. The Thai guards on the other side seemed to have good relations with the Japanese, as they were heard laughing and joking with the patrol. The escapees returned and remained hidden in thick jungles near the border. They decided against attempting a crossing as they were likely to be caught on the other side and handed back to the Japanese Military Police with dire repercussions.

They continued hiding for a number of days, unsuccessfully trying to find a way to cross into Thailand. Swarms of mosquitoes made life very uncomfortable and there was the constant threat of contracting malaria. To make matters worse, the escapees neither had passports nor the money to acquire them from the authorities. As their patience and supplies were running out, they decided to take a final plunge to try and get across the international border into Thailand, before they were assailed by some form of sickness and could not travel any further.

Thus on 19 May, they started early to attempt the crossing. At about 11 AM, as they were approaching the border near Kuala Nerang, they heard urgent shouts behind them. Instead of turning back, they sped up and broke into a run, but sharp cracks of rifle fire over their heads halted them in their tracks. They turned around and raised their hands. Angry members of the Japanese patrol quickly caught up with them and the fuming soldiers cuffed them soundly on their heads with fists and rifle butts. They fell to the ground and lay still while the soldiers kicked them in their ribs.

Parab had somehow managed to hang on to his huge hat all this while. Once on the ground, he deftly extracted the precious map and pushed it deep down the front of his shirt. The three officers were roughly hauled to their feet and taken to the nearby border check post at Padang Besar. All the while, they kept pleading their innocence and feigned ignorance about the location of the border.

Luckily, the Japanese border guards believed their statements and released them after another sound beating, but not before rudely searching them and confiscating their precious anti-malaria quinine and water sterilizing tablets. This was a serious setback as malaria and dysentery were rampant and none of them could afford to fall ill during the escape. Besides, Captain Ramaniah, MO, had procured the precious Quinine tablets with considerable difficulty.

Despite the close call, they continued hiding in the wet jungle near the border for more than a fortnight. The humming mosquitoes and leeches made life miserable. Woefully short of food and water, the escapees realized that they had to move on to avoid recapture.

In desperation, Pritam remembered that Dogar Singh had told him that they could easily obtain passports in Penang and have them stamped as well. As they had failed to cross the international border, they decided to go to Penang and try their luck. That very evening they took a train to Penang, and on getting off, they went to the Government Office near the jetty. Here they met an Indian clerk who listened to them sympathetically and told them to come again the next day. They stayed overnight at the local Gurudwara and went back the next morning. The clerk proved helpful and they managed to get the required passes that were written in both English and Japanese, and were valid for a period of three months. The passes had been made out for them to visit their relatives in Bangkok. It all seemed too good to be true!

While at Penang, Balbir was recognized by a Sepoy of 4/19 Hyderabad Regiment who was now running a shop there. He informed them that a VCO of the unit named Subedar Diwan

Singh had taken refuge in the nearby INA Camp. The three went to the INA Camp and were fortunate to meet the VCO.

Diwan Singh had escaped from the 9 1/2 Milestone Fatigue Camp about a fortnight earlier. And like them, he too failed to cross the border and proceed to Thailand. However, he seemed to have suffered a nasty experience, for when the three offered to take Diwan with them, he just refused and said that he was quite comfortable where he was and did not want to attempt another border crossing. He seemed to have lost all desire to return to India.

The trio also chanced to meet two other Indian commissioned officers—2nd Lieutenant Mathur and 2nd Lieutenant Trilokekar—and a sepoy named Risal Singh. Both the officers and sepoy were from the Royal Indian Supply Corps (RIASC). Surprisingly, none of the IA personnel they met at Penang were keen to return to India. The trio returned to Alor Setar by train and again went and hid themselves in the deep jungle.

Next morning, Pritam led the others back to the Gurudwara and contacted Dogar Singh, who took their passes to a Japanese officer he knew for verification, and asked them to meet him later.

But the following day Dogar Singh had some bad news. There had been a major altercation between the Japanese and Thai authorities. As a result, the Thai authorities were refusing to accept passes issued by the Japanese side. Dogar also added that in order to cross the border and travel in Thailand, they would now require Thai passports, in addition to the Japanese travel papers they had obtained in Penang. The three officers were dejected and annoyed at Dogar Singh for not telling them earlier about the necessity of obtaining Thai passports. They were very disappointed and felt that their trip to Penang had been an utter failure and a waste of time and effort.

With little or no hope left of legally crossing the border, all three agreed to take a calculated risk and once again illegally try and cross over into Thailand. Luckily, during one of their surreptitious visits to Alor Setar town, the officers came to know of a Sikh farmer named Ujagar Singh, who frequently crossed the border with a loaded bullock cart. Supposedly he knew the guards well on both sides of the border.

The officers gingerly approached the farmer, who agreed to take them across the border for a fair sum of money. The scoundrel even wanted to have some money paid to him in advance! With a crafty smile, the farmer said that he would cover them with hay and take them across the border in his bullock cart.

Although there were plenty of nagging doubts about the farmer's integrity, in their desperate condition, the escapees decided to take the risk. After all, Dogar Singh did vouch for the farmer and also gave them a letter of introduction for him. The three held a detailed discussion, and after taking the decision to cross the border illegally, on 21 May the escapees cautiously entered Padang Besar. They were careful after their

Thailand-Malaya border, Singapore and Sumatra

previous unpleasant experience. They found a vendor to change their money into Thai currency and quickly returned to their jungle hideout.

The next day, 22 May 1942, was a big day for the three escapees. They silently left their jungle hideout and went to meet Ujagar Singh who had arrived with his bullock cart at the designated spot. With pooled financial resources they paid the farmer the advance sum of money that he wanted for surreptitiously conveying them across the border into Thailand. He then made them lie down in the bullock cart with their small bundles of belongings and deftly covered them with bundles of loose hay. He warned them not to talk or move, and then cracked a small whip.

The bullocks and cart jerked forward, its wooden wheels creaking loudly. Ujagar Singh walked along on one side of the cart. Lying hidden below the hay, the trio had many anxious thoughts, and they literally froze when they heard loud voices of Japanese guards at the border crossing point.

The three escapees lay unmoving beneath the hay, knowing that they had no chance of escape if the guards decided to prod the hay with their long bayonets. Luckily, the guards joked with Ujagar Singh and conducted only a random search of the upper bundles of hay. The escapees lay unmoving underneath and their doubts about the farmer's integrity eased when they heard Ujagar Singh joke first with the Japanese and then with the Thai Border Guards.

"*Bandeyoh, chup-chaap chhipe raho, hilna nahin,*" he said loudly to them in chaste Punjabi, as he took the bullock cart safely across the border.

Once the cart was well-hidden in the jungle on the Thai side, the three officers emerged from the hay and happily jumped to the ground. Removing the loose strands of hay that were sticking to their clothes, they profusely thanked the smiling farmer and happily paid him the remainder amount of the agreed money. Then they picked up their bundles and melted into the jungle. The three were delighted to be in Thailand, which was not officially under Japanese occupation!

The officers had heard during their train journeys that Thai customs officials often carried out a strict checking of documents on trains running between Konge and Hadyai. Unfortunately, they had not found anyone willing to stand surety for them nor did they have enough money to get the required passports from Thai immigration authorities. A Thai passport would have cost them 210 tikals as they had gathered. Thus, they had no option but to risk travelling in Thailand without documents, and instead of boarding a train, they decided to walk to Hadyai.

After trudging for a night and a day on wooden sleepers below the metal rail tracks, they cautiously entered the Hadyai Railway Station. The platform was practically deserted at that time since it was almost midnight. They passed the remainder of the night sitting on wooden benches on the platform. There were about 30 Japanese soldiers sitting together on the platform, with their rifles placed nearby in a stack.

In order to appear like nondescript civilians, the escapees separated and individually went to the small booking window to buy rail tickets to the coastal town of Prachu-ab-Khirikan, on the east coast of Thailand.

In the morning, they boarded a train heading to Bangkok, and sat in different compartments to avoid any suspicion or detection. As the train began to move and pulled out of Hadyai, they heaved a sigh of relief.

The train chugged along the narrow Thai peninsula and passed the stations of Bandoh and Chumporn. While the train was passing Chumporn, they saw a large group of about 60 enemy soldiers sitting on the platform apparently waiting for a train.

On 27 May, they reached the small town named Prachu-ab-Khirikan, on the east coast of the narrow Thai peninsula. There were many Japanese soldiers camping in the open area in front of the railway station. A number of Japanese soldiers were also camping on the railway platform.

As the escapees were quietly leaving the railway station, an aircraft flew low over the town. Instinctively, the officers nearly dived for cover before stopping themselves and laughing heartily. They had almost forgotten that they were in neutral Thailand and it was a Thailand Air Force plane on a routine sortie.

Jungle Crossing to Burma

A man can be destroyed but not defeated.

—*Ernest Hemingway, The Old Man and the Sea*

At Prachu-ab-Khirikan, they were sheltered by a benevolent, old Pathan named Khan Zaman, who was married to a Thai woman, and ran a meat shop in the town. The Pathan and his wife lived near the town and owned a number of cattle. The couple had a playful little daughter who was fascinated by the strange looking travellers.

As they talked of the Indian region of Punjab and the North-West Frontier, they gained Zaman's confidence, and he hesitatingly began to disclose his colourful past back in India. He told them that he had committed a murder in his native land and was wanted by the British authorities. The Pathan had fled to Calcutta and on to Burma. From there he had moved to this remote Thai town as a fugitive. He now ran a meat shop, but earned his livelihood by smuggling cattle to and from Burma—an occupation in which he was well versed!

[Nearly 47 years later, in 1989, Balbir returned to Singapore and retraced his journey along the escape route. He met and thanked most of the people, or their descendants, who had assisted them in the escape. At Prachu-ab-Kirikhan, he was saddened to learn that both Zaman and his Thai wife had passed away. However, he met their daughter and they joyfully recounted the old times. The daughter, now a middle aged woman, told Balbir that it had been rumoured that they were captured in the jungle and shot by the Japanese. She was happy to learn that they had reached India safely and she celebrated the event by inviting Balbir to dinner.]

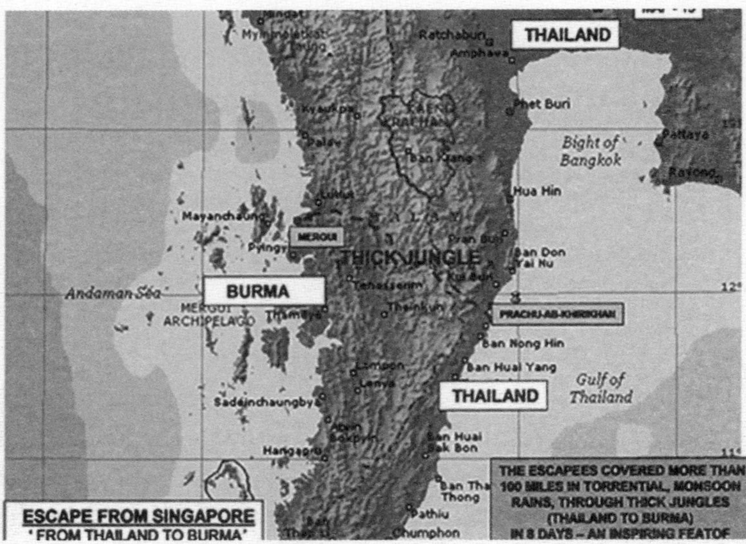

Map showing jungle route from Thailand to Burma

When the escapees told Khan Zaman they wanted to go to Burma, he told them about hidden jungle trails that crossed the inhospitable terrain into Burma. He, however, warned them that traversing the hundred miles or so to Burma was extremely difficult, even in good weather conditions. The first day's march would take them to a small village at the edge of the deep jungle. Then, the difficult part of the journey would begin. As monsoon rains were already lashing the area, the Pathan urged them not to follow the jungle trails to Burma. He knew the area well and insisted it was a suicidal venture with monsoon in full force.

Faced with a difficult option, the escapees reviewed their future plans. On seeing their sorry plight, Khan Zaman even offered them the choice of staying on at Prachu and working with him. He said they could easily get married and settle down to a fine life. Zaman assured them cattle smuggling was a lucrative business and soon they would be rich young men. Considering the uncertain times, it was a tempting offer! However, their status as IA officers and the burning desire to reach India made them refuse the offer. They were willing to face the risks of travelling to Burma along the jungle trails, if they could finally get to India. After they had made up their minds, they informed Khan Zaman.

With a heavy heart, the crusty old Pathan allowed them to leave his home. Zaman's kindly Thai wife wrapped some food for the journey in banana leaves and made small packets bound with thin bamboo shavings. Zaman even sent a servant-boy named "Kaka" and another Thai young man to act as their guides for the first few days of their difficult journey to Burma.

After leaving Khan Zaman's residence, the small group of five individuals walked the whole day over narrow and meandering paths. As the sun was going down, they neared a village in the foothills at edge of the jungle. Kaka and the Thai young man spoke to the village elders in front of a large thatched hut. After an animated discussion, the group was taken upstairs and made comfortable for the night. They were even given a hot meal of rice and lentils.

When the villagers had left, Kaka chuckled and said that the village elders had been impressed when they were told the three escapees were accomplices of Khan Zaman and well-established professional cattle lifters. Kaka had also said they were proceeding to Burma by the jungle route to bring back a large herd of stolen cattle and would leave some cattle at their village!

Next morning, before leaving the village, the escapees convinced the overawed villagers that they were indeed cattle lifters. With difficulty, they controlled their laughter at the new-found respect that the profession of cattle lifting had earned for them. After a crisp farewell, the three escapees followed Kaka and the young Thai lad to the nearby foothills.

Though Kaka had been boasting about his knowledge of the route to Burma, he could not lead them on to the proper track. But as he had been living with Khan Zaman and looking after his cattle and taking them out for grazing, he had some knowledge of the area. He soon found the entry point to the deep jungle, beyond which supposedly lay the jungle route to Burma. Kaka and his companion said hurried goodbyes and happily returned to Prachu-ab-Khirikan and Khan Zaman.

The monsoon rains had set in and the leeches and mosquitoes turned the trek into a terrible nightmare. The danger of wild animals and merciless dacoits added to their woes. The old Pathan's description of the perilous route could not have been more accurate. The escapees often wondered if they had made the right decision to follow the jungle route. All along this route to Burma they encountered the most difficult conditions they had ever experienced in their lives. Only one thing seemed positive and kept them going—they were heading towards India and now there was no turning back!

With sheer grit and determination, the tired and famished officers plodded on in incessant rains and often lost their way in the thick jungle. Initially, a group of inquisitive monkeys followed them and swung overhead from the tall branches and chattered shrilly. When the escapees walked into the dark and silent primary jungle where even the sun's rays never entered, the monkeys turned back. The stench of rotting wood assailed their noses as they trudged through this part of the jungle.

Though they never spoke out aloud, each officer was aware of the grave dangers that lurked around them. The torrential monsoon downpour made movement most difficult and at times they could barely see one another in the heavy mist. They soon lost all track of time. However, they marched on and were determined to succeed. To overcome their fears and fatigue, they would loudly sing a song as they trudged deeper into the silent jungle. Words of the song in Hindustani were, "*Chal, chal re naujawan, door tera gaon, aur thake paon. Rukna tera kaam nahin, chalna teri shaan. Chal, chal re naujawan ....*" The song spurred them on and they could forget their travails for a while. Having taken the difficult decision to move by the jungle route, they vowed to either reach Burma or perish in the difficult venture!

In this manner they trudged on through the for bidding jungles. When they halted for the night, Balbir would collect firewood and help Parab with the cooking of rice and lentils. Pritam would scout around and find a safe spot for the night. He would build a small shelter with sticks and leaves pulled off the surrounding trees. Invariably, the heavy rains would leave them soaked to the skin and it was difficult to find dry firewood for lighting the cooking fire. As they lay down to sleep in wet clothes, swarms of ants would come crawling over them and cover their skins with painful bites.

Around a couple of days after leaving the village, they were all of a sudden surrounded by some mean-looking cattle-lifters, just as they began to cook their evening meal. Six or seven men stood around them while another two or three men remained in the dark with about 20 head of cattle. The cattle-lifters wore dark-coloured clothing that had been drenched in the rain and they had dirty scarves tied around their heads. They wielded nasty looking *dahs* and large knives. The trio were lined up against some large trees and bodily searched in a rough and rude manner. Initially, the cattle-lifters took away all their medicines but threw them down in disgust, as they could not read the labels in English or decipher their usage.

Loud words and fingers placed on their lips spelt a solemn warning for the trio to stay silent. After the warnings, the cattle lifters departed as silently as they had arrived. With the stolen cattle, the criminals headed in the direction of the village. The escapees were shaken by the incident and knew they were extremely fortunate to have survived. However, they vowed to be more careful in the future and Pritam was positioned as a look-out, while Balbir and Parab cooked the meals.

It was now maybe three days since they had left the village. A fast-flowing stream obstructed their path, and suddenly, while attempting to cross it, all three officers were swept away by a raging torrent. They managed to survive by desperately clinging to roots that were protruding from the banks. However, all their belongings, including the precious quinine tablets, were washed away in the flow. Soaked to the skin and panting from exhaustion, they helped each other to safety atop the slippery bank. They were tired, terrified and all hope seemed to be lost. However, after a good rest, they recovered enough strength and spirits to resume their onward trek.

After walking for a while, the trio realized that they had repeatedly passed the same trees and other landmarks. They had a strong suspicion that they had been going round in circles and could be lost in the forbidding jungle. In their weary state, as they hacked their way over steep slopes and along overgrown and unfamiliar tracks, their fears continued to grow. Soon, they were certain about going round in circles and sure they were lost. In their exhausted state, the situation seemed utterly hopeless.

Since long they had run out of the food packets that Khan Zaman's kindly Thai wife had provided for them. They were on the verge of collapse due to starvation, and were plagued with terrible hallucinations. The escapees began to harbour visions of a sad and lonely end in deep jungles on the Burma-Thai border.

Nearabout the fifth day saw them sitting huddled together in the dense undergrowth when the most unbelievable thing happened. They heard the unfamiliar sounds of dogs barking and a cock crowing—sure indicators of a nearby human habitation! After the time spent in the silent jungle, they thought their ears were playing tricks in their exhausted state. But when they sat still and listened carefully above the constant hum of jungle insects, they could even hear the excited shouts of children. With great joy they realized that the sounds were indeed real and not a figment of their weary imagination. It was too good to be true and seemed like a gift from heaven.

With renewed energy, they followed the sounds and soon staggered into a small jungle clearing with a couple of thatched huts. Half-naked children shrieked in amazement and ran back as the strangers broke from the jungle. Dogs barked wildly and the startled villagers stared in wonder as the three dishevelled figures staggered into the jungle clearing and collapsed from sheer exhaustion. They appeared to have walked in from another world! The simple tribals offered them a sumptuous meal of hot rice, delicious lentils and ripe bananas. It was a lavish treat after the frugal meals they had been having during the time in the jungle.

They warmly thanked their hosts and slept fitfully in one of the huts that was raised above the damp ground on four stilts. The good food and rest suitably revived the officers. Inquisitive children overcame their fears and sat with the escapees. They were fascinated by the officer's beards and some of the children even ventured to touch their faces. The escapees wanted to stay longer in the welcome surroundings of the jungle village and rest their weary bodies, but the harsh reality of their status as escaped prisoners forced them to continue with their journey. They did not want the friendly villagers to face the wrath of Japanese Army for helping in their escape.

On the next day, they warmly thanked the hospitable villagers and disappeared into the thick jungle once again. Before leaving the village, Balbir had given the excited children a peacock feather that he had been carrying in his pocket. He told them in Hindustani that he prayed the feather would bring them good luck. He did not know whether they understood him or not, but the eldest boy shyly stepped forward and took the feather. The other children had clapped happily at the impromptu presentation.

Some days later, on 5 June 1942, and again in a state of extreme exhaustion, they limped into the outskirts of Tabolick in Burma. Bone-tired and extremely hungry, they thumped each other on the back—they were proud to have made it to some civilization. They felt truly wonderful to be alive and finally in Burma. Wide smiles cracked their tired faces. They sank to the ground and inhaled the wonderful smell of damp grass.

However, their problems were far from over. Burma was on the frontlines of the ongoing war and heavy fighting was raging between the Allied and Japanese forces. Due to the proximity of frontlines, the Japanese troops were generally alert and present in larger numbers. But, for the moment, the pleasing feeling of having reached Burma blocked out all fears that lay ahead. Their primary needs of hunger and sleep were so over-powering that nothing else seemed to matter.

The old Pathan's deadly predictions of doom had not come true and the impossible had been achieved by the trio. They had traversed more than a hundred miles through forbidding jungles in eight days, surviving torrential monsoon rains and fast-flowing jungle streams! It was truly a tremendous feat of human endurance, even for physically fit and well-nourished soldiers. Instead, the feat had been accomplished by three escapees who were in a ragged physical and mental condition. They had succeeded because of their dogged determination and the burning desire to reach India.

At Tabolick, they saw a derelict tin-mine called *Tabolick Tin Dredging Company* and decided to change their identity as clerk, store-man and overseer at the Tin Mine. From Tabolick, they happily went by a country boat to Mergui via Tenasserim.

On the country boat they sat on seats made of wooden planks. A middle-aged and seemingly well-educated Indian sat next to Pritam. After brief introductions, he asked if they worked for IIL. When they replied in the negative, he started up a lively conversation. He told them he worked in a store in Bangkok and was on his way to Mergui, to see if his wife and her parents were alright. He had not been home since the Japanese had occupied Burma. When Pritam asked him about the conditions in Thailand, the Indian said that at the beginning of the war, the Thailand government did not treat Indians well. However, through the mediation of Swami Satya Nand, matters had improved and now there were lesser restrictions imposed on Indians. He said that at heart, the Thais were already tired of the Japanese, who wanted to have everything done in their own way, without reference to the Thai authorities. The latter had to keep silent for fear of being persecuted by the Japanese military forces in direct control of the land.

Referring to the recent air crash in which Swami Satya Nand, Giani Pritam Singh and Captain Akram Khan of INA had reportedly been killed, he said that it was known to all Indians, and the Thai authorities too, that the air crash had been engineered by the Japanese. It had been done because the Japanese did not like Satya Nand's straight talking. The Thai

Prime Minister had great regards for the Swami and he had wept when he heard the sad news of the air crash. It was said the Thai Prime Minister was not in favour of the Swami going to Japan. He would have prevented it if the Swami had left from Bangkok, but he had been powerless as the party had left from Singapore. The Swami had done valuable service for the Thai government—he had added to their vocabulary, written books on Thailand and closely fostered the cultural relationship between Thailand and India.

He further said the Indians in Thailand thought of Swami as being very outspoken, someone who talked straight with the Japanese when discussing the issue of Indian independence. This was the main reason he was not popular with the Japanese and they wanted to get rid of him. The feeling among the Indians was that the Japanese were only concerned with conquering India. Their concerns about India's independence were really a farce. His eyes were bright with emotion, and he anxiously looked around to confirm that he wasn't being heard by others on the boat.

At Mergui, they were examined by a suspicious Burmese police officer and a couple of constables when they passed themselves off as employees of the Tabolick Tin Dredging Company. The officer's suspicions seemed to grow as the mine was a derelict. However, Pritam handled the tense situation splendidly by confidently saying that the mine was re-starting its operations from the month of July with new staff members. The police officer, however, was not convinced and asked them to get someone to vouch for them.

Not knowing what to do, the escapees confidently walked towards the nearby marketplace with the Burmese policemen following closely behind. Luckily, they found an Indian provision shop at the beginning of the market and quickly entered the store. Throwing caution to the wind, Pritam rapidly told the astounded shop-owner in Hindustani about their status as IA officers who were being tailed by the police. They prayed and hoped fervently that the shop-owner understood the language or all would be lost. Seeing the shopkeeper nod his head, Pritam added that they had told the police officer a concocted story of working at the Tabolick Tin Mine, and requested him to vouch for their good character. The police officer and his men had followed the escapees into the shop and the showdown began. The shop-owner nodded when the police officer said something in authoritative and rapid-fire Burmese. The three escapees simply stood beside the shop-owner smiling innocently. The officer scowled and said something more to the shop-owner. Apparently disgusted by the way things turned out, he swung around on his heels and left the shop in a huff followed by his men.

Once the police had departed, the shop-owner smiled and told them his name was Prem Chand and they were lucky he knew fluent Hindustani. He added, continuing in Hindustani, that he had just given a guarantee for the three of them as being known men of good character.

Over a welcome cup of hot tea, he explained how to travel to Tavoy. He warned them to be wary of dangerous dacoits who infested the area. He also mentioned that he had heard there were Australian prisoners in POW Camps at Mergui, Ye and Tavoy. The escapees thanked Prem Chand profusely and left his shop feeling grateful that they had been saved. If Prem Chand had not come to their rescue, the Burmese police officer would surely have handed them over to the Japanese and it would have been all over for them. It also did not escape their observation that at Mergui, the bulk of the traders and shopkeepers were extremely scared of the Japanese. When asked the reasons for this strange behaviour, Prem Chand had told them with a smile that whenever the Japanese required labour, they asked the public to provide manpower or to pay money in lieu, so that manpower could be hired.

From Prem Chand's shop they proceeded to the jetty. On the way, they saw many ragged Burmese soldiers straggling in the streets. The Burmese seemed to be running their own government, but were in effect functioning under close Japanese supervision. After a good rest, they moved from Mergui on 15 June and travelled by a motor launch, followed by boat and bus. They reached Tavoy on the evening of 16 June, and walked through the dark streets to reach the local Gurudwara.

The Gurudwara at Tavoy was packed with refugees squatting on the floor and some who were asleep on the first floor. After the Japanese occupation, it appeared that many people had decided to stay on at Tavoy. They would proceed to Rangoon or Pegu after travel conditions had improved. The refugees told the three escapees that the area between Tavoy and Moulmein was inhabited by merciless dacoits who were hostile in the best of times. With the uncertainties of war-time, the dacoits were expected to be even more dangerous. The area was close to the Thai border and it was somewhat of a no-man's land. Some well-wishers among the refugees dissuaded the escapees from going further along the route to the north without joining a larger group. When the latter asked people in the Gurudwara to accompany them to Central Burma, no one wanted to go along that route till it had been cleared for safe travel. The three escapees weighed their chances and then took a decision to go ahead on their own.

The Government of Lower Burma had been entrusted to the Thakin Party by the Japanese. The Thakin Party was decidedly anti-Indian and a number of checks had been enforced on the movement of Indians. The escapees learnt that Indian passengers were required to obtain a pass before they could buy a ticket to leave Tavoy. Despite their lack of passes, on the next day they boarded a crowded bus to Yeh. They asked for tickets and were told to show their passes. The conductor was a considerate man and he permitted them to sit in the bus. But he told them the bus would be halting at the police station and they could obtain the required passes to purchase bus tickets. The bus started up and soon made its routine stop at the police station where all the passengers alighted and went inside where a rotund and bespectacled Japanese officer sat with his interpreter at a large table.

The interpreter asked the trio their names, what they did, why they were going to Rangoon and how long they expected to stay there. They, in turn, confidently replied that they were working with the Tabolick Tin Dredging Company and proceeding to Rangoon to meet their relatives. They added that they were worried about their relatives' safety because of the war and required passes to buy bus tickets. Their replies were translated by the interpreter and the Japanese officer nodded and seemed to be satisfied with their explanation. They were asked to wait for five minutes and then given the necessary permits to leave Tavoy. Bowing and profusely thanking the Japanese officer, they left his office. Outside, they boarded the bus and bought tickets after producing the permits. The conductor gave them an "I told you so" look and smiled condescendingly.

Shortly after the bus left Tavoy, it crossed two ferries. At each ferry there was a detachment of Japanese soldiers guarding it. Thereafter, the road was good and the bus moved ahead with speed. They reached Yeh on the evening of 18 June. As they had been doing all along, they stayed in the local Gurudwara of Yeh. There was a railway line from Yeh to Moulmein, but trains were not plying on the line as a bridge had been destroyed in the fighting. So, on the morning of 19 June, they set off from Yeh and walked for 22 miles along the railway track to Lamaing.

This part of their journey also proved extremely tough as they had to walk on jagged stones of the railway track. Torn shoes and painful blisters on their feet added to their miseries. Hostile people living near the railway track were a constant menace. One village on the railway line was particularly dangerous. They were warned at Yeh to stay away from these people. They could not forget the horrified looks on faces of some refugees, of South Indian origin, when they recounted their terrible story of being waylaid on the railway track between Yeh and Moulmein. The refugees had been robbed and some of them were even murdered by the bandits in the group of hostile villagers. The surviving refugees had fled and saved their lives.

As they walked past the village, the trio felt the burning animosity of the villagers who were sitting in front of their huts all along the railway line and staring at them. The three officers rapidly moved along without either looking back at the villagers or stopping to talk with them. The villagers barely got any time to organize themselves and harass the escapees. The trio increased their speed by taking larger steps on the stony surface and even broke into a run after they had passed the village. In great pain from their badly bruised feet, they staggered into Lamaing in the dark. They stayed the night at Lamaing and left the next day by train.

They had had enough of walking for a while and their relief was unimaginable as they sat in the swaying railway carriage. Through the carriage windows they glimpsed the beautiful, blue-green waters of the Andaman Sea and the Bay of Bengal. It was a heady feeling to know that the shores of India lay across the cool waters that they were seeing. But they knew that a long and tricky journey still lay ahead. They were yet to cross unknown territories occupied by the enemy forces. Most of the railway bridges were built on thick wooden supports and trains went over them with a deep clattering sound. The escapees continued their journey by train and reached Moulmein on 24

June 1942. On the way, they saw many Japanese military trains pass by them at high speeds both during the day and night. The trains were generally loaded with old lorries, equipment and horses.

At Moulmein, both Captain Pritam Singh and Captain Parab fell ill. Parab had a high fever and was admitted to a convent hospital run by Eurasian and European nuns. Also they wondered why, in Moulmein, was there an exceptional fear of the Japanese. Finally, an Indian shopkeeper cleared the mystery. He told them that all large and small shopkeepers of Moulmein had been jailed for two days and made to do hard manual labour because they had discontinued the value of 10 cent notes in *annas* and *pice*. Once again, Pritam and Balbir stayed in a Gurudwara and waited for Parab to recover his health.

Their money had almost run out and they knew that more would be needed soon to continue with their journey. They approached one Arjan Singh, a rich shop-owner and wood contractor who had a few elephants. They were astonished when, on being asked to lend them Rs 50, Arjan Singh reached into his pocket and offered them only Rs 5. They felt humiliated and declined to take the money.

At the Gurudwara, they met four soldiers belonging to 8 Burma Rifles. All four individuals were living as civilians ever since their unit had disintegrated after the Japanese occupation of Burma. They told the escapees that treatment of prisoners-of-war in Moulmein was bad. The food comprised of only rice and salt and the prisoners were all in rags. These four soldiers and another civilian also wanted to go to India and they had some money. So they all agreed to join the escapees and the group left Moulmein on 30 June and arrived at Martban by a ferry-boat.

On the ferry-boat they encountered a bunch of four stragglers from a unit of 8 Gurkha Rifles that had been overrun by the Japanese in Burma. The Gurkha soldiers were silent and subdued, but they seemed glad to be in the company of the three IA officers. They all proceeded together by rail, bus, ferry-boat, on foot along the rail tracks, and by bicycle-rickshaws to Pegu via Thaton.

They arrived in Pegu on 2 July 1942. The bridge over Sittang River had been destroyed in the fighting and all movement across the river was being conducted in country boats. The stretch of railway line between Thaton and Bilin was patrolled by armed policemen on a rail trolley to ward off dacoits. The group stayed in Pegu for a day or two and moved on to Rangoon. The Japanese were in occupation of Burma and they had a series of escapades as they evaded many enemy check-posts.

As they walked into Rangoon on 4 July 1942, a flight of US bombers droned towards the city in broad daylight. The city was rocked by massive explosions and a number of buildings were reduced to rubble. The streets were deserted and only a few locals and Japanese troops were visible. The rest of the party with whom the three officers had travelled decided not to continue to India thus leaving the escapees again in dire financial difficulties. The three escapees stayed in the Gurudwara at Rangoon.

There were another 30-40 people staying at the Gurudwara at that time, and some of them appeared to have a suspicious behaviour. They were forever hiding their identity, and the escapees were worried they could be Japanese agents. Therefore, they approached Gurdit Singh, who was the Gurudwara Chairman and a member of the India Independence League (IIL), and told him that they had to leave urgently because of business interests. Despite his protests, they moved to another Gurudwara at Manigaon (Prome Road), about three miles out of Rangoon. Gurdit Singh even offered to obtain employment for them, but they politely refused.

While at Manigaon, Pritam twice went to Rangoon to visit the IIL Office. Having lost their cards earlier, they again joined the IIL by paying Rs 1 each. The membership enabled them to purchase railway tickets after giving a letter of recommendation to the Station Master.

While at the IIL Office, Pritam heard a great deal of propaganda, including people saying that an INA contingent numbering between 70,000 and 90,000 men would soon march into India.

Returning after his second visit, Pritam came across a Japanese staff car parked on a street corner. An Indian-looking driver was standing next it and he hailed Pritam in Hindustani. Pritam stopped next to him, and the driver told him with a smile that he had been a sepoy in the IA and was now the driver of a Japanese officer. He surprised Pritam by asking if he had come from Singa pore. Feeling that the sepoy might have recognized him, Pritam feigned a coughing bout, mumbled incoherently and then rapidly walked away shaking his head.

At the Gurudwara, they met an amicable Sindhi merchant, who they felt could be taken into confidence and asked for some money. They told him how their financial problems were hindering their travel to India.

The Sindhi merchant proved to be a die-hard nationalist who understood their problem and voluntarily gave them Rs 200. This windfall temporarily resolved their financial woes. They also met an ex-Sub Inspector of Police at the Gurdwara, named Pritam Singh (hereafter called PS to distinguish him from Captain Pritam Singh), who lived at Monywa. He told them that he had tried to get back to India but could not succeed. So after his failed attempt, he began conducting trade between Rangoon and Monywa. PS promised to accompany them to Monywa, and informed them that in order to trade in Burma, everyone had to have a "Business Pass". Since such a pass could prove useful during travel, PS said he would help them obtain the required Business Passes with their IIL Membership Cards.

Despite having IIL Membership Cards and a recommendation to the Station Master, the three managed to purchase train tickets from Rangoon to Mandalay with great difficulty.

Once they had the tickets, they went from the Gurudwara at Manigaon to the railway station at Rangoon on 9 August and boarded an evening train to Mandalay. PS accompanied them on the journey. Strangely, the Gorkha stragglers were unwilling to go any further and stayed behind in Rangoon.

Ordeal at Monywa

> Courage is not merely a virtue; it is the virtue. Without it, there are no other virtues.
>
> —*Field Marshal Sir William Slim, Courage and Other Broadcasts*

The train journey ahead was uneventful. The ticket inspector came and checked their tickets. As they proceeded north, many more Japanese troops and military vehicles were visible. The train reached Mandalay in the morning. PS, who had been very helpful to them as he was fluent in Burmese, also knew the area well. From the Mandalay railway station, he took them to the bus stand where he bought tickets for Monywa, and they boarded a crowded bus. The bus drove into Monywa just as it was getting dark. From the almost deserted bus station, PS guided them through the darkened streets to the local Gurudwara.

Several people were living in the Gurudwara, and many more came and went all day long. PS knew the Granthi named Natha Singh, and he introduced the escapees as his friends. He explained to Pritam and the others that many people were stranded in Monywa due to heavy fighting taking place towards India. While at the bus station they had also met a Bengali Ayurvedic doctor who was, strangely enough, called "Babuji-Babuji". A shop-keeper near the Gurudwara told PS that they had to be careful as there were many suspicious people in Monywa, who could be either British or Japanese spies. He warned them again to be very cautious.

Their plan now was to go to Kalewa and then enter India. However, people at Monywa advised that it would be quite impossible to cross the Japanese check post at Kalewa unless they had a Pass. They, therefore, applied to the Japanese authorities for a pass to proceed to Mawlaik, and onward to Kalewa. They met a Japanese Intelligence officer—Lieutenant Nomi—to get the necessary passes to go to Mawlaik. He spoke good English and asked them what they did for a living. They told him they were businessmen who owned two shops in Pegu. Displaying a forlorn look, they added that their parents had left for India in March, but were held up in Mawlaik. Since they were concerned about their parents, they wanted to bring them back from Mawlaik. Lieutenant Nomi asked them to come back after a few days.

When they went back, they found that the case had been shuttling between several Japanese offices ever since it had been submitted. It had last been forwarded to the Burmese authorities—the *Jijikhai.* The concerned Burmese office now said that their papers had been returned to the Japanese authorities. In exasperation, Balbir told Lieutenant Nomi they were worried about their parents and would be grateful for written instructions on how to proceed in the matter. To their horror, on the next day, they discovered that their case had been re-submitted to the *Jijikhai!*

They were helped by one Mr Pillai, a former Public Works Department overseer, who was living about 600 yards from the

Gurudwara. They chanced to meet Pillai near the Gurudwara and told him about their predicament. Pillai listened carefully and said he would try to help them out. He operated quickly and could obtain permission from the *Jijikhai* for them to proceed to Mawlaik, but they still had to obtain the final approval from the Japanese. Pillai accompanied them to meet Lieutenant Nomi, who appeared quite annoyed to see them again. He asked them to see him after an hour. Lieutenant Nomi must have gone over the case, for he immediately announced that he could give them only two passes to proceed to Mawlaik. The third person would have to stay at Monywa and remain there as a hostage and report daily to Nomi.

They could scarcely believe what they just heard. Balbir asked Nomi for permission to go out of the office and discuss the matter amongst themselves. Nomi had already begun to peruse another file, and without looking up, he dismissed them with an annoyed wave of his hand. They trooped into the verandah outside the office and began to analyse the shocking information. They felt there was some spiteful reason why the Japanese did not want them to proceed to Mawlaik. Disgusted with the attitude of the authorities, they felt there was no use of again meeting Nomi. Instead, they silently set off for the Gurudwara without exchanging another word between them.

At the Gurudwara, they met PS who had come to meet Natha Singh, the Granthi. They narrated to PS all that Nomi told them. He heard them out patiently and surmised they should not shelve their plans, as they had not been officially debarred from travelling to Mawlaik. He added he knew an Indian trader named Thakur Singh, who could help them go to Mawlaik as he knew some Japanese officers in Monywa. PS promised to take them to Thakur Singh's house the very next day.

Early the next morning, PS was at the Gurudwara. He took them to Thakur Singh's house through some narrow streets.

Thakur Singh warmly welcomed them into his home and prepared hot tea for them to drink. PS said he had some work in town and left after having tea. The host sat with the escapees and discussed their proposed move to Mawlaik and Kalewa. He showed a great deal of interest in the details of their plan to reach India. He told them he knew some Japanese officers who could grant them the necessary permission to go to Mawlaik and Kalewa.

After discussions, he asked them to relax in his house while he went out on urgent business. The escapees were immensely pleased with their good luck and settled down on the comfortable easy-chairs. In no time at all, they were fast asleep. They did not know how time flew. After an hour or so Thakur Singh was back with soldiers of the *Kempeitai*—the secret Japanese Military Police—who roughly roused the escapees from their deep slumber.

The three escapees are captured by Japanese Kempeitai (Secret Police) at Monywa (Burma)

The *Kempeitai* arrested them before they could attempt a getaway. While being led away, the three realized how the Indian trader had betrayal them so terribly. They felt sickened and cursed themselves for trusting a rogue with their plans. Thakur Singh spoke with the Japanese soldiers on friendly terms, and he apparently knew them well. He avoided the escapees' gaze and slipped out of the house while they were rudely manhandled. The Japanese soldiers bound their wrists and took them to the Monywa police station.

On arrival at the police station, their wrists were untied, and they were made to sit on the flagstones of the verandah floor with their few possessions scattered around them. A single Japanese soldier was left to guard them while the others went inside. Not wasting a minute, Parab asked the guard and went to the latrine. Here he quickly destroyed his documents.

Meanwhile, Balbir requested the disinterested guard to allow him to prepare tea at the small fireplace, or *chula*, at the end of the verandah. On the pretext of taking out tea leaves from his bundle, Balbir removed all incriminating documents, including a precious diary he had been maintaining since their escape from Singapore. Looking over his shoulder to ensure the guard was not watching him, he burnt the incriminating documents in the fire that he lit, ostensibly to prepare tea.

Having destroyed the documents, he offered the guard a steaming, hot cup of the beverage. The other guards soon returned and conducted a rough, body search. They also searched their bundles carefully, in which they found a letter written in Hindi that had been given by Prem Chand in Mergui to Parab, for posting in India. They also found a rough, hand-drawn, sketch map of Akyab and a small account book in Gurmukhi. The map happened to be a portion copied from a map of Burma by Balbir while at the Chartered Bank in Rangoon.

Fortunately, the guards could read neither Hindi nor Gurmukhi. They dismissed the incriminating letter, and the accounts notebook, as documents of little consequence. The sketch map did not have any notations; it too, was discarded by the guards as a piece of trash. At the end of the search, the guards were puzzled at not finding any other incriminating documents or maps. The prisoners were interrogated and constantly threatened with death by beheading or the firing squad. Questions asked during the interrogation indicated that the Japanese were looking for undercover Allied agents and informers, who had infiltrated into Burma through the front-lines. They did not seem interested in escaped prisoners who were heading towards India.

During the initial round of interrogation, the three officers stuck to the story they had concocted. The trio acted dumb and insisted they were innocent refugees who owned shops in Pegu. Their parents, parted from them during the fighting, had proceeded towards India and were last known to be in Mawlaik/Kalewa. They were now desperately looking for their parents. After saying so, Balbir promptly extracted the plastic-covered photograph of Captain Jaswant Singh of Royal Dutch Army and thrust it before the Japanese interrogator saying softly and sadly, "My father!"

The *Kempeitai* were not inclined to waste time on such half-wit and scruffy looking civilians, who appea-red to be genuine refugees despite the Indian trader's vehement protestations. Thakur Singh bent down low before the *Kempeitai* and kept repeating that all the three individuals were Indian agents. The escapees were thrilled to see the trader receive a few punches around his ears from the annoyed Japanese interrogating officer. Also, their joy knew no bounds when they saw Thakur Singh rudely sent on his way from the police station with a well-directed kick in his pants!

After interrogation, all three were placed in cramped, solitary confinement cells located at the rear of the police station. Once inside their cells, they softly called out to each other and were glad that they could communicate. However, their joy was short-lived, as the Japanese armed sentry strode before each cell and conveyed that they were not permitted to talk to each other. He put a finger on his lips and tapped his rifle to indicate the consequences if they spoke with one another. The prisoners silently surveyed their little cells and discovered, to their horror, deep finger-nail scratches on the cells' walls. The lines bore mute witness to tortures that must have taken place in the solitary confinement chambers.

The deep lines on the walls greatly frightened the escapees during their incarceration. However, the daily interrogation and beatings left them little time and energy to contemplate on the fate of the earlier prisoners.

The interrogations continued, but the trio kept repeating their story. The Japanese seemed to accept their concocted story generally. However, they were not satisfied with two issues. First, they repeatedly asked about the location of the shops in Pegu. Second, they did not understand why the trio could not speak Burmese, despite being owners of two shops. The escapees had decided on false locations of the shops in Pegu and hoped that the Japanese would not be able to cross-check facts. About their not knowing the Burmese language, they had told their interrogators they were sent for public school education to Singapore at a young age. They had lived in a "boarding school" and were given English medium education. Though the Japanese officer was suspicious about their not knowing the Burmese language, their fluent knowledge of written and spoken English gave credence to their claims.

On 14 September, the officer-in-charge of the police station summoned all three prisoners. They were surprised to see Lieutenant Nomi also lolling on a chair next to him. Nomi seemed to know about their arrest and details of their interrogation. He told them that they were being put on a train to return to Pegu the very next day. He added that they would be given the necessary documents and that they must not return to Monywa.

The prisoners' relief was unimaginable. After being locked-up and tortured in the *Kempeitai* chambers for nearly a fortnight, the three officers found it hard to believe they were to be released, unharmed, from Japanese custody.

Home, Sweet Home!

> See, the conquering hero comes!
> Sound the trumpets, beat the drums!
>
> —*Judas Maccabeus, A Chorus of Youths*

The next day, the three escapees bowed low and smiled humbly while bidding farewell to the unsuspecting Japanese guards who herded them to Monywa railway station. There they were given permits that allowed them to travel back to Pegu. When the train arrived, the Japanese guards unceremoniously pushed them into a compartment. The guards departed only after the train had chugged out of Monywa. The escapees, not in a mood to follow orders, jumped off the train at the first stop after Monywa and worked out their plans.

They had learnt of large-scale Japanese troop movements towards India, and it appeared to them that significant enemy operations were afoot in that direction. After the nasty experiences in Japanese custody and their providential release, they did not wish to be caught up in the fighting. If caught again, they were likely to be recognized by Japanese troops and executed. Fearing increased Japanese troop activity, they altered their plans to go directly to India. Balbir and Parab wanted to give Monywa a wide berth and avoid the Japanese build-up at the front-lines towards Tamu. They had also heard of American and Chinese troops operating in the north. So they wanted to proceed north to Myitkyina and beyond and contact the Allied Forces there.

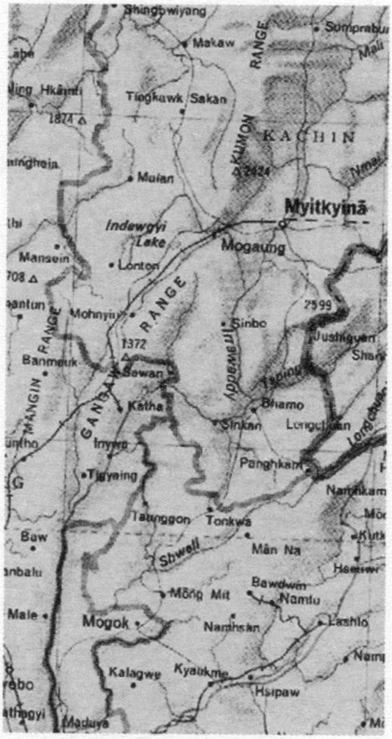

Map of North Burma

However, Pritam felt that proceeding to the north and crossing front-lines would be far too dangerous, due to jungle fighting that was taking place in that area. Besides, they knew that there was steep terrain in the north, with mountains and vast swathes of unknown territory.

After the unpleasant interrogations and physical torture by the Japanese at Monywa, the three of them realized the difficulties involved in putting together a credible story for their interrogators to accept. They realized it was impracticable for a group of three members to successfully continue the escape. Thus, the group mutually decided to split into two parts.

It was a sad parting as Pritam volunteered to proceed to India all by himself via Tamu. Parab and Balbir parted company with him very solemnly, after hugs and warm hand-shakes. The date was 15 September.

Without a backward glance, Pritam walked down the track leading to the left side. Watching Pritam depart, Balbir said quietly to Parab, "There goes our lone wolf! I wonder what the future holds and may God always be with him".

Pritam had come into their lives in the Singapore POW camp like a breath of fresh air! As a member of the escape team, he was hard-working and tough, always with a bagful of new ideas to tackle any problem they encountered. All through their travels, they had observed that Pritam instinctively loved to work by himself. Balbir was right when he compared Pritam with a lone wolf. Seeing Pritam depart—alone, voluntarily and fearlessly—both Balbir and Parab began moving along the heavily-jungled northern route to Myitkyina and beyond to India. They were to seek their fortunes along the challenging "northern route", hoping to contact the Kachin Levies, the US Forces of General Stilwell, or the Chinese forces descending from the north.

During one of his talks with PS and the others, Pritam had heard of a small Indian community and Gurudwara at a mini-township named Chhangu, about 15 miles from Monywa. Having walked for a short distance, he proceeded to Chhangu by a local bus. Balbir and Parab had worked out an arrangement before parting to re-join Pritam in case they had severe problems or found the relatively unknown northern route difficult to negotiate. Pritam was to stay at Chhangu till

20 September for any word from the others. If he did not hear from them, he was to continue to Tamu.

The bus Pritam took was crowded with locals who were carrying pungent and over-ripe fruits and vegetables to sell at Chhangu. There was also a Burmese man carrying a basket load of cackling and fluttering chicken, and he held onto the basket with great care. The short ride soon ended, and Pritam got off the bus at the central market of Chhangu. It was a colourful marketplace teeming with people as it was the "market day" and people had brought local produce and livestock to sell. At the marketplace, Pritam asked for the way to the Gurudwara and was told it was located nearby. He walked on as directed and soon reached his destination.

Waiting at the Gurudwara, by 20 September, Pritam still had no word from the other two escapees who had gone north. At Chhangu, he also came in contact with another IA officer named Captain Mahabir Singh Dhillon, who had joined the INA. Over various conversations, Pritam learnt that Dhillon was being sent by the Japanese to India to recruit *fifth column* agents for the INA's planned advance into India. So Pritam decided to accompany Dhillon, and together they walked towards the active frontline.

Carefully avoiding both the Japanese and Allied picquets and the incessant artillery fire, they moved cautiously on foot through the battle zone and proceeded to Kindat and Tamu.

Finally, they contacted a picquet held by a platoon of Rajputana Rifles Regiment. Here they met one Captain MacDonald who received them well and spoke to his superiors over a field telephone. MacDonald arranged guides for them to pass through IA defensive positions safely.

After a day of walking, on 25 October 1942, they reached HQ 29 Infantry Brigade. From there, they both proceeded to India.

Once in India, Pritam and Mahabir formally surrendered to the British. During the subsequent preliminary interrogation sessions, Pritam gave details of the escape and told the interrogators about Captain Balbir Singh and Captain GS Parab, and their plan to travel north to Myitkyina and contact the Allied forces. This information was quickly relayed to troops of the Allied forces in the general area of Fort Hertz. They were asked to look out for two escaped prisoners in their areas and not shoot them dead on sight.

Racked with malaria, stomach ailments and grossly underweight, Captain Pritam Singh was thankful that he had finally reached his homeland. Six long, torturous months spent as a fugitive in enemy territory were over. Supreme determination and courage had helped him to cover nearly 2000 miles across hostile jungles and through vast Japanese-held territories. He was among the first survivors to reach India after the fall of Singapore, and he gave a first-hand account of the Japanese occupation forces in Malaya and Burma.

Captain Pritam Singh was driven to Manipur Road (now called Dimapur) railway station from where he boarded a train to Calcutta. For the next couple of days, he had a chance to sleep and relax while a steam locomotive hauled the meter-gauge train to Calcutta. When he was not sleeping, he looked out of the window of the comfortable first-class train compartment. Pritam was intrigued by a framed map on the wood-panelled wall above the steel wash-basin. He sighed when he remembered the decrepit trains in which they had travelled while journeying through Malaya, Thailand and Burma. How he wished they had had such a map to consult during their travels through Japanese-occupied territories. During waking hours, Pritam would look out of the window, and his mind wandered back to the harrowing times undergone in bitter battles in Malaya and Singapore, and their escape from the POW Camp.

It was dark when the train pulled into the well-lit and busy central platform of Calcutta railway station. Innumerable soldiers from different parts of the world could be seen moving about, wearing different service uniforms—soldiers from India, Africa, Britain, Australia and the USA. Walking amongst the soldiers were tall members of the Military Police, moving in pairs in step with one another. Two nursing orderlies received Pritam and guided him to an ambulance car parked at a corner of the large parking lot. A few more ambulances were standing in the parking lot. Serious battle-casualties were being carried from the train on stretchers and loaded into the ambulances.

At the large Military Hospital (MH), Pritam was admitted in the Officers' Ward. There were Eurasian nurses on duty, who issued him with a grey-coloured flannel night-suit. A team of doctors examined him. He had a light dinner and was given medicines for fever, malaria and dysentery. An antiseptic ointment was applied on his painful feet, and they were bandaged. He spent the next twelve days at the hospital in Calcutta in recovery. Owing to the wholesome diet he was fed, he quickly added some weight to his wasted frame. When the MH finally discharged him, he took a train to Delhi.

As the war situation with Japan was highly volatile in 1942, Pritam was initially suspected of being a member of the INA, who had been infiltrated into India by the Japanese. While talking to his interrogators, he was relieved to learn that both captains Balbir Singh and Parab had been found in the thick jungles to the north, in the area of Fort Hertz. During his detailed interrogation sessions, the British wanted to know the locations and strength of Japanese troops he had seen at various places during the escape. He mentioned the following locations and the approximate number of enemy troops he had seen:

Singapore	between 15,000-25,000
Penang 5,000	Alor Setar 1,200
Mergui 400	Tavoy 200
Moulmein 1,500	Pegu 1,500
Rangoon 10,000	Monywa 2,500

Pritam's interrogations convinced the authorities that he and the others had actually escaped from Singa-pore, and they were not Japanese agents! Their incredible story of escape and subsequent travels spread like wildfire, and kept the authorities spellbound. Pritam never knew when the interrogations turned to casual debriefings. But he discerned a softer attitude and observed a positive change in the nature of questions asked. He also noticed that there was no longer a guard outside his room, and he was free to walk around the premises.

Soon, he was permitted to write letters to his family. Officials had earlier on informed his family that the Japanese had captured the three escapees and shot them dead by a firing squad. This disinformation had been spread by the Japanese to dissuade others from escaping. Military Intelligence had received such reports from their operatives in Singapore, and Army HQ had duly informed the officers' families. Thus, on receiving the letters, Pritam's family was thrilled, and the arrival of all three officers in India was indeed a very happy occasion.

For their daring escape from Singapore, Captain Pritam Singh, Captain Balbir Singh and Captain GS Parab were awarded the Military Cross in February 1943 by Lord Linlithgow, the Viceroy in India. The presentations were made during a glittering parade at the large square on Kingsway (now called Vijay Chowk on Rajpath). Later, the three officers also received congratulatory demi-official letters from Field Marshal AE Wavell, Commander-in-Chief in India.

In due course, the newly-promoted Major Pritam Singh, MC, decided to avail some long-leave after his perilous exploits and lengthy trek to India. While he was on leave, his parents arranged a match for him. The prospective bride's parents lived in the city of Dehradun, and Pritam got married at a small Gurudwara in Rajpur there. After the wedding, he spent some happy days at Dalanwala, a part of the beautiful city of Dehradun.

Little could anyone anticipate the brewing war into which Pritam would plunge, shaping the destiny of a people as well as his own.

Mrs. Balbir Singh, Khanna, Bahadur Singh, Shrinagesh
Bhagwati Singh and Pritam Singh

Mrs Pritam Singh (first from right)

Onwards to Kashmir

When placed in command, take charge.

—General Norman Schwarzkopf

After the end of the world war, India continued to pass through turbulent times as wheels were set in motion by the British to leave after granting independence to the country. A new nation was to be carved out of the western portion of India and named Pakistan. East Bengal was also to be included in Pakistan, and it was to be an Islamic country. The Indian Army too would be divided based on the religious identity of the troops. Officers had to either opt for the Indian Army or join the newly-formed Pakistan Army.

On its arrival from Java (Indonesia), 1 Kumaon was stationed at Pulgaon. They had been selected for the role of a Parachute Battalion and had handed over their duties to 5/8 Punjab Regiment.

On 6 November 1946, the unit left for Malir Cantt, near Karachi, to join the 2 Airborne Division. It reached Malir on 11 November 1946, after travelling by train via Nagpur and Delhi. At Karachi, 1 Kumaon, under the command of Lieutenant Colonel GB Beer, presented a splendid guard of honour on 22 March 1947 to Lord Louis Mountbatten when he arrived as the last Viceroy of India. It was a time when most British officers were leaving India for the UK. 1 Kumaon did its basic parachute training at Chaklala near Rawalpindi, and converted to a Parachute Battalion. However, the parachute training occurred at a rather slow pace.

On midnight of 14-15 August 1947, two independent nations—India and Pakistan—came into existence, each with their respective armies.

1 Kumaon (Para) became part of the Indian Army and was brought to New Delhi by its CO, Lieutenant Colonel GB Beer.

Crest of 1 Kumaon (Para)

In October 1947, Pritam, accompanied by his wife, went to Delhi. He was still on leave when, on 30 October 1947, he happened to drop in at Army HQ, South Block, at around 5 PM. He found scenes of intense activity with most lights turned on in the impressive South Block building.

On enquiring about the reason for the heightened activity, officials told him that tribal *lashkars* from the North-West Frontier Province (NWFP) had been sent in by Pakistan to invade Jammu and Kashmir (J&K).

The tribal raiders were beefed-up with regulars from the Pakistan Army. Pakistan, in its defence, had said that some regular troops on "leave" may have voluntarily joined the tribal raiders. Muslim personnel of most J&K State Force Battalions had deserted and joined up with the tribal raiders.

Maharaja Hari Singh of Kashmir wanted Indian forces to intercede and help his State Forces. India had told him that it could assist only if the state of J&K acceded to India. Thus, Maharaja Hari Singh signed the Instrument of Accession, by which the state of J&K merged with the Indian Union.

Shortly after that, on 27 October 1947, the first Indian infantry battalion had flown from Delhi to Srinagar. The first batch of troops to arrive in Srinagar was the battalion headquarters and three companies of 1 Sikh under Lieutenant Colonel Ranjit Rai.

161 Infantry Brigade, under Brigadier JC Katoch, was now tasked with defending Kashmir, and 1 Kumaon (Para) too was ordered to fly to Srinagar. But before the unit could proceed, Lieutenant Colonel Beer had to be relieved as only Indian nationals were allowed to proceed to Kashmir.

At around 9 PM the same evening, Pritam was handed an official order to take over command of 1 Para (Kumaon) in the rank of Lieutenant Colonel. The order also stated that the unit was to proceed to war in Kashmir.

With the order in his hands, Pritam immediately went to Willingdon Airport and took over the command of 1 Para (Kumaon). At 5.30 AM the next morning, he took off for Srinagar along with his unit, leaving his wife to find her way back to Dehra Dun.

As there were few transport planes with the then Royal Indian Air Force (RIAF), civil aviation companies like Kalinga Airways of Biju Patnaik were requested to provide DC-3 (Dakota) aircraft to ferry troops and their stores to Srinagar.

Lt Col GB Beer

Lt Col Pritam Singh, MC, on assuming command of 1 Kumaon(Para) at Delhi on 30 Oct 1947. [Note the Paratrooper's Wing affixed on his right sleeve]

No one knew at that time whether the airstrip at Srinagar was safe for landing, or the raiders had captured it. The pilots displayed incredible enthusiasm and courage and kept inducting troops and stores on this strip, which had no navigational aid and no Air Traffic Controller. There was a time during the rapid landings when nothing was visible due to the dust raised by the last plane that had landed. But the planes kept flying and kept landing on the dusty airstrip, disembarking troops.

Troops of 1 Kumaon (Para) on landing at Srinagar – 31 October 1947

After 1 Sikh, 1 Kumaon (Para) under Lieutenant Colonel Pritam Singh, MC, became the second infantry battalion to be flown to Srinagar. When the Battalion HQ and two companies landed at Srinagar on the morning of 31 October, the situation was rather grim. The enemy was again on the move after pillaging Baramulla, and they had contacted the 1 Sikh position at Pattan, about 16 miles from Srinagar. After landing, Pritam immediately sent Major UC Pant with "D" Company of 1 Kumaon (Para) to Mile 9 on the road from Srinagar to Baramulla. A fair-weather road from there branched off to Gulmarg.

Pritam correctly appreciated that a part of the tribal *lashkar* that was advancing from Baramulla would be sent over the high Pir Panjal range of mountains to threaten Srinagar airfield. Another two companies of 1 Kumaon (Para) flew into Kashmir the next day to join the battalion at Srinagar, followed by the fly-in of 1 Punjab and "D" Company of 4 Kumaon under Major Somnath Sharma.

"D" Company of 4 Kumaon fought a bitter battle with these raiders at Badgam on 3 November and saved the vital airfield. During the battle, Major Somnath Sharma, the company commander, was killed and the company suffered heavy casualties. Before he was killed, Som sent the following historic radio message to his Brigade HQ at the Srinagar Airfield, "... we are surrounded and heavily out-numbered. The enemy is only 50 yards away. I will not withdraw an inch, but will fight to the last man and last round."

The raiders were defeated, and the airfield saved. Major Somnath Sharma was posthumously awarded India's first Paramvir Chakra (PVC). That very evening, 1 Kumaon (Para) had its first casualties. Tribals ambushed their convoy of three civilian lorries killing three other ranks (ORs) and wounding one OR.

A Headquarters Jammu and Kashmir Force was created and located at Jammu to coordinate the battle for Kashmir. Major

General Kalwant Singh became its commander and was made the overall in-charge of the operations. He arrived in Srinagar on 5 November.

Lieutenant Colonel Pritam Singh, MC, with Major General Kalwant Singh (photograph taken later at Poonch)

Battle of Shalateng

You cannot manage men into battle. You manage things; you lead people.

—*Grace Hopper, Admiral, US Navy (retired), Nova (PBS TV), 1986*

Brigadier LP Sen replaced an injured Brigadier Katoch as commander of 161 Infantry Brigade and decided to redeploy his troops. 1 Sikh was pulled back from Pattan to Mile 4, near Shalateng. On 5/6 November, "A" Company of 4 Kumaon under Major HS Bolina was redeployed with 1 Kumaon (Para). The unit moved to the Rifle Range Area with orders to attack the enemy concentration from the southern flank. 1 Kumaon (Para) under Lieutenant Colonel Pritam Singh, MC, along with 1 Sikh, and "A" Company 4 Kumaon with air support from the RIAF (Royal Indian Air Force), literally massacred the tribal *lashkars*. Air recce and attacks also took place on the long line of more than a hundred lorries and buses of the tribals. The tribals were seen in large numbers between Shalateng and Zainakut.

Brigadier Sen used the "A" Company of 4 Kumaon to secure the FUP, while 1 Kumaon (Para), 1 Sikh, two Daimler Armoured Cars of 7 Cavalry and RIAF aircraft attacked the tribals most ruthlessly on receipt of codeword "GO". Pritam had tactically positioned himself on a small piece of raised ground next to the road. He had good observation here and could read the engagement and pass orders to his troops. He rose to his feet and directed the Kumaonis and Sikhs to assault through the fields in extended line. The troops advanced and fired at the fleeing raiders. LMG fire ripped through the surprised enemy raiders, while RIAF aircraft dived with their machine guns blazing. The attack was a great success, and the tribals were routed in the ploughed fields of Shalateng.

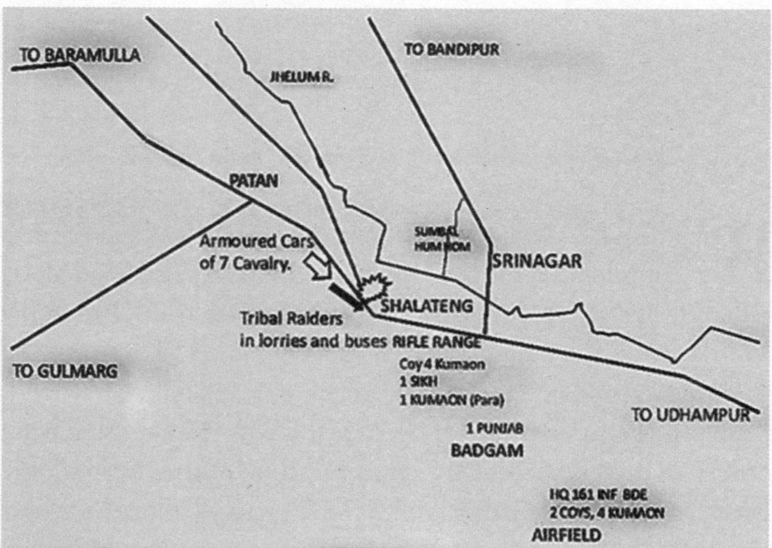

MAP-BATTLE OF SHALATENG (NOT TO SCALE)

The *lashkars* suffered heavily, and over six hundred got killed. Most of their civilian lorries and buses burnt fiercely after being strafed and bombed by the diving RIAF aircraft. The terrified tribal survivors ran pell-mell towards Baramulla and Uri to save their lives. Within thirty minutes of the commencement of automatic firing by the ground troops and air attacks, it was all over for the raiders. Those surviving raiders who ran desperately towards the road to Baramulla hid behind a line of thick bushes that lined the fields.

Daimler Armoured Car

As they fled, the raiders bypassed the armoured cars that stood deployed in their path. However, on Pritam's signal, the armoured cars swung around their turrets and engaged the fleeing raiders causing more casualties. The deep stutter of their heavy machine guns created untold panic. For a long way, past the fiercely burning vehicles, the road to Baramulla was soon littered with Pathani sandals and looted possessions hurriedly discarded as the raiders fled in utter disarray.

This historic victory at Shalateng saved the capital city of Srinagar in the very nick of time and changed the fortunes of Kashmir. The battle was a turning point in the Pakistan-sponsored tribal invasion of Kashmir. It was a very significant victory for India. Unfortunately, Lieutenant Colonel Pritam Singh's great contributions during the Battle of Shalateng are often overshadowed by the later events at Poonch. During this historic battle, Pritam was the senior-most officer present on the battlefield, and he had a major role in comprehensively defeating the raiders and achieving the overall victory. 1 Sikh, 1 Kumaon (Para) under Pritam, the Armoured Cars support under Lieutenant Noel David and the RIAF aircraft had resolutely defeated the tribal raiders and caused them to flee.

It is worth recording here that Pritam was the chief architect of Pakistan's overall defeat during operations in J&K (1947–48). His resounding victories, first at Shalateng and then at Poonch, defeated the grandiose plans of a belligerent Pakistan. It came to be known later that Pakistan had launched the tribal invasion of J&K with the covert support of some officials of the British Government.

After Shalateng, 1 Kumaon (Para) was at the vanguard of the Relief Column (161 Infantry Brigade under Brigadier LP Sen) that was in pursuit of the fleeing tribals. At Mile 54, the fleeing raiders paused to set fire to the power station to permanently destroy this source of electricity to Kashmir Valley. But before they could do so, the Kumaonis arrived. They fought a fine action with the raiders and put them to flight. With this action, Pritam saved the power station at Mahura. On resuming the advance, the Relief Column safely reached Uri. After taking Uri, the column was ordered to relieve Poonch where the J&K State Forces garrison was under siege and attack by the raiders.

Thus, on the morning of 20 November 1947, this column of Daimler armoured cars of 7 Cavalry, 2 Dogra and 1 Kumaon (Para) set off on the route from Uri to Poonch. Although the road condition was poor, by nightfall, the main column had reached below Haji Pir Pass. The rearguard, consisting of two platoons of 1 Kumaon (Para) and 24 vehicles, was delayed due to mechanical failures in some vehicles and had to spend the night at Milestone 7.

The next morning, tribals ambushed the delayed rear-party and made concerted attempts to cut the convoy into two parts. Sixteen men of 1 Kumaon (Para) got killed, and fourteen were wounded. The Pathans looted the ambushed column and set fire to the unit's lorries.

Despite the thirty casualties that his unit suffered, Pritam resolutely broke through the raiders cordon and pushed on to Poonch.

The Pathans then burnt a large wooden road bridge at Milestone 5, and all movement to Poonch stopped temporarily. Quickly repairing the burnt bridge, the remainder of 1 Kumaon (Para) was also able to advance and enter Poonch on 21 November 1947 with 419 men.

Poonch Under Siege

> I would define leadership as the will to dominate, together with the character which inspires confidence. A leader has got to learn to dominate the events which surround him; he must never allow these events to get the better of him; he must allow nothing to divert him from his aim; he must always be on top of his job, and prepared to accept responsibility.
>
> —*Field Marshal The Viscount Montgomery of Ala-mein,*
> *Military Leadership*

All the high hills surrounding Poonch were at that time in the hands of the raiders and the Pakistan Army, and no other obstacles separated the antagonists. Besides the native population of the town, there were over 40,000 ill-clad, starving, and panic-stricken refugees, many of whom were sick and wounded. They had all converged at Poonch after the raiders had ravaged their towns and villages in the countryside.

Pritam thus faced a big dilemma when he arrived there. With the increased population, the available food stocks were estimated to last for barely a week. He had to urgently find a way to increase the stocks of grain in town.

Approximately 1,400 J&K State Force troops had withdrawn under pressure from various border towns like Mirpur, Kotli and Jhangar, and assembled at Poonch. They had no heavy weapons and the ammunition with them was down to a few rounds per rifle. The enemy held all the cards, and the dice was heavily loaded against the defenders. All set to descend on the town of Poonch, the raiders wanted to loot, rape and massacre. The J&K State Forces garrison had begun preparing their withdrawal, condemning the refugees to certain death. However, providence intervened, and one man arrived to turn the tide. Pritam immediately cancelled the orders for withdrawal of the J&K State Forces and took charge of the defences. The arrival of Pritam and his men proved once again the veracity of Napoleon's maxim that in war, it is not the men that count, but only the "man".

Leading a handful of his Kumaoni troops, who yelled the most blood-curdling war cry, Pritam commenced assaulting the hills above Poonch, which had been occupied by the enemy. This audacious and plucky act so completely unnerved the raiders that they fled away in panic, leaving behind weapons and ammunition scattered all over the hills, and allowed the townspeople to get supplies in. At this point, no one had an inkling that the town would remain besieged for more than a year. In the months to come, the raiders would repeatedly occupy the hills as it provided them with maximum domination over Poonch. Pritam would frequently conduct these guerrilla attacks on the raiders in the long months of the siege, as the latter were desperate to take Poonch. But before all this played out, the higher HQ sent instructions for the troops to prepare to withdraw from Poonch.

The message of withdrawal somehow leaked out, resulting in a pall of gloom engulfing the entire town. The horrors that befell the inhabitants of Mirpur, Kotli, Baghand and scores of other towns flashed through the minds of those who had escaped from these places and found refuge in Poonch. Correctly sensing the feelings of the people, and as a true patriot, Pritam responded to his higher authorities by saying that abandoning the population of Poonch and refugees would be the greatest betrayal. The Army would forever forfeit the trust of the nation. He would instead go down fighting with his garrison than have the Tricolour lowered at Poonch.

The mountains of the mighty Pir Panjal Range, tower above the Poonch Area

Pritam was just the man Poonch needed in the hour of its greatest peril. Later on, he recorded: "On arrival, I found the State Forces garrison preparing to evacuate from Poonch, and it took me some time to make them realise that I intended to stay and that there would be no scuttling."

With great skill and daring, Pritam set about reorganising the Poonch defences and restoring order and administration in the town. Instinctively, the troops and the population knew that a great leader had arrived. His highest-priority task was to organise rations for the permanent population of Poonch and the multitude of refugees who had converged there for safety. That, and to construct an airstrip to remain in touch with the outside world.

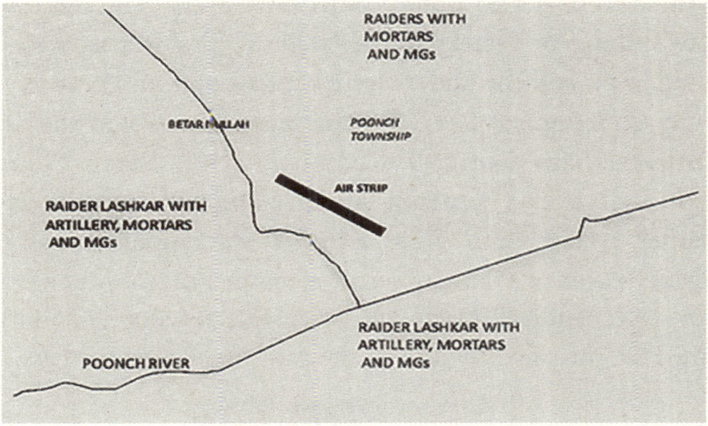

Sketch of Poonch Area and Airstrip

The airstrip was a vital necessity to receive reinforcements, arms and ammunition, and evacuate the sick and wounded. After carrying out a detailed reconnaissance for site selection, and considering technical factors such as approaches for landing and take-off, it was decided to construct an airstrip between Betaar Nala and Poonch township. It was a busy time for Pritam and his ad hoc staff when the airstrip construction began on priority. As word spread, men, women and even children came out in their thousands to help in the construction efforts. They began to pull down buildings that came in the way of the runway, clear the debris and fill a part of the large nullah bed. Civilians often worked under a great deal of enemy fire from the surrounding hills. Pritam had galvanised the citizenry and infused in them a new spirit of defiance and sacrifice.

To feed the large number of people lodged in Poonch, Pritam started raiding the surrounding villages that were under enemy occupation, to obtain food grains and livestock. In this way, a total of 90,000 *maunds* of grain was collected during the year-long siege. Often there were casualties during these raids that depleted the strength of the Poonch Garrison.

These were hectic times, and nearly every day, there was acute sniping or attacks by the raiders. The attacks were all beaten back, and the raiders were kept away from Poonch.

On 6 December 1947, Pritam was promoted to the rank of Brigadier. His Second-in-Command (2IC), Major Dharam Singh, took over 1 Kumaon (Para) in the rank of Lieutenant Colonel. Major Pran Nath Kaushik was appointed as the Brigade Major of Poonch Garrison under Pritam. Much later, in the 1965 India-Pakistan War, Kaushik, serving in 1 Punjab (Para), fought gallantly during the capture of Haji Pir Pass.

Major Pran Nath Kaushik

The airstrip was soon completed, and on 12 December 1947, the legendary Group Captain "Baba" Mehar Singh, DSO, accompanied by Air Vice Marshal Subroto Mukerjee, carried out a daring trial landing in a Harvard aircraft. On the same afternoon, the first DC-3 Dakota aircraft landed on Poonch airstrip, carrying with it a complete section of 25-pounder artillery guns and ammunition.

After that, the fledgeling RIAF began what they called *Poonching,* by courageously flying through the narrow river valleys, to safely reach Poonch. An air bridge using the Dakota aircraft was created, first by day, and later on, even by night.

The air bridge flew-in supplies and flew-out refugees, despite constant interdiction by Pakistani mountain artillery guns.

Brigadier Pritam Singh, MC (left) with Air Commodore Meher Singh, DSO, after a successful trial landing at the newly-constructed Poonch airstrip, Dec 1947

Checking newly-arrived ammunition at the Poonch airstrip, Dec 1947

Pritam mounted attacks almost daily on the raiders, who were occupying most of the heights around Poonch. He used troops of 1 Kumaon (Para) and even the J&K State Force Battalions. Often there was heavy fighting, and they sustained many casualties. Most of the wounded were evacuated to Jammu by the returning aircraft, where they received necessary medical treatment.

With the sick and wounded refugees who were to be flown out

After the sound defeat at Shalateng, the raiders aim of capturing Srinagar had been severely negated. And now, their frustrations rose because they were unable to capture Poonch! Stiff resistance by the Indian garrison had significantly hurt their cause. Still the invaders and their Pakistani mentors were determined to take Poonch and subject its population to rape, murder and looting. The wily raiders intensified their attacks with renewed vigour. But Pritam, the valiant Indian commander and his small band of brave soldiers, stood firmly with the citizens of Poonch and countered every move.

There was an urgent need for more troops to keep the enemy at bay. Therefore, Pritam raised two Militia battalions (later named 8 and 11 J&K Militia) from among the able-bodied men at Poonch. These troops had a sound knowledge of the terrain, and they fought well along with the other regular troops.

Refugees being loaded in a Dakota aircraft, to be flown out of Poonch, Feb 1948

During December-January of 1947/48, 3/9 GR was flown into Poonch. The arrival of another infantry battalion vastly improved the overall availability of trained soldiers.

However, in February, the enemy attacked Khanetar Ridge causing heavy casualties and pushed back 1 Kumaon (Para). The unit left behind many dead, wounded and weapons. Reportedly, the Commanding Officer Lieutenant Colonel Dharam Singh, and his Adjutant had thrown away their weapons to remain unencumbered for their speedy withdrawal. Later, they both blamed this grave loss on their respective orderlies. This shameful act by principal officers of the unit seriously affected the morale of the troops.

The enemy continued with its desperate efforts to capture Poonch. So great was their urgency to capture Poonch that mountain artillery guns were surreptitiously brought forward to the heights around the township and airstrip. Suddenly, artillery shells began to explode around Poonch and on the runway of the vital airfield. The enemy was resorting to direct fire from the artillery guns. The firing severed the air link and caused serious casualties amongst the residents. Pritam realised the situation had once again become desperate, as it had been when he had arrived in Poonch. The enemy artillery fire would have to be stopped immediately to allow the airstrip to function.

To add to the immense problems facing the Poonch Garrison, on 21 March, Pritam was wounded. A rumour quickly spread that he had died. Because of the great adoration that existed for Pritam, this report went around Poonch like wildfire, spreading fear, chaos and panic through the town. Pritam quickly realised that harmful effect of the spread of this unfortunate rumour. Though he was still suffering from the ill-effects of his wounds, he wanted to quash this rumour at the earliest. So he asked to be propped-up in a jeep and driven around the streets of Poonch. Seeing that he was alive gave the people solace and helped put an end to the rumours of his death.

By now, the higher authorities knew about the use of artillery guns by the raiders to target Poonch leading to the closure of the newly-made airstrip. They also knew about the wounds suffered by Brigadier Pritam Singh. So they promptly issued another message instructing the garrison to save itself from further losses and to prepare to pull out from Poonch. Pritam, though still confined to his bed, would not hear of it. Once he was able to walk, he led attacks and drove the enemy beyond the direct observation of the airstrip and Poonch township. The raiders could save their guns only by physically hauling them back to their new positions. But from these positions, the Pakistani artillery guns could not directly target either the airstrip or Poonch township with observed, direct artillery fire. With 1 Kumaon (Para) and two companies of J&K Militia, Pritam fought a superb action against the raiders and re-captured Khanetar Ridge.

In April 1948, Sheikh Abdullah and Bakhshi Gulam Mohammad flew in and visited Poonch. Sheikh Abdullah addressed a public meeting in which he chided the refugees for killing Muslims during their escape from the raiders. The people were shocked by what he had just said. There was hardly a refugee in that audience who had not lost a family member and suffered extreme brutalities at the hands of raiders. Instead of giving them a word of sympathy, Sheikh Abdullah condemned the hapless refugees. The angry crowd promptly drowned his words, and bitter slogans rent the air. With great difficulty, troops intervened and were able to save the Sheikh and his party. However, they had to be packed off in the first available aircraft, though a bit unceremoniously. The memory of this ignominious departure from Poonch must have haunted Sheikh Abdullah and later caused him to side with the many detractors of Pritam.

In May 1948, Major General Atma Singh took over command of Jammu Area Division from Major General Kalwant Singh (sadly, Atma was to die later in a road accident while travelling to Udhampur). From the very beginning, a frosty relationship developed between Atma and Pritam. Since Atma was now in overall command of regular operations being conducted by Pritam around Poonch, he took some faulty decisions that were tantamount to inviting disaster.

Why he took an instant dislike towards Pritam is not clear—possibly because of the latter's fine career as a professional soldier and outspoken mannerism to "achieve his end". But the flawed decisions taken as a result were to have far-reaching consequences. Atma took away 1 Kumaon (Para) from under the command of Pritam at Poonch and ordered the unit's return.

The only other regular infantry battalion now remaining at Poonch was 3/9 GR. However, this unit had recently suffered a severe operational setback, and its morale was low. Pritam took the decisions by his immediate commander in his stride, even while he kept hitting out gallantly at the enemy, and kept them away from Poonch.

At that time, returning leave parties, about 300 in number, were at Jammu awaiting an airlift to return to Poonch. On orders of General Atma, these troops were held back as the "division reserve" for operations that were taking place for the "link-up" with Poonch. This decision clearly showed the derision with which Atma viewed the operations being conducted by Pritam at Poonch. It was an unfortunate military decision by the GOC and his staff. For they knew that units at Poonch had suffered heavy casualties, and were battling the enemy at half their strength.

As 1 Kumaon (Para) began preparing to leave Poonch, Pritam received reports that the battalion was carrying valuables from the local palace. Sometime earlier there had been a letter to Pritam from the Army Commander instructing him to ensure the safety of the property of the Rajah of Poonch. Therefore, Pritam ordered a search of the luggage of 1 Kumaon (Para) while it was being loaded in the aircraft. People often say in hindsight that Pritam committed a cardinal error of command, to order a search of a departing unit's baggage. However, the decision to search the unit's baggage reflected Pritam's "no-nonsense approach" in such matters, and his strict adherence to the Army Commander's directions contained in the letter.

Notwithstanding the background of reports that mentioned about pilferage of the Rajah's property, there appears to have been no justification for subjecting the battalion to a search. To thus humiliate troops who had followed Pritam through the very fires of hell and beyond was sacrilege. These were brave men who had taken such heavy casualties without a word, had covered themselves with glory and accepted hardships of the long siege with great stoicism. The search recovered only one ivory-handled cane and two shooting sticks from the CO's baggage, a few silk cushions from the Subedar Major's box, and two old table fans from the QM. But this action turned the battalion against Pritam. Atma was to exploit these injured feelings of the troops to the maximum.

A relieving force under Brigadier Yadunath Singh had assembled at Rajauri. This force was called the Rajauri Column. It eventually grew to be division-sized, comprising 5 and 19 Infantry Brigades, as well as the original Rajauri Column, and its task was to link-up with the beleaguered garrison at Poonch. The force had with it supporting field artillery and two troops of Sherman tanks of the Central India Horse. The code-name of the operation was *Operation Easy*, to make the complex operation appear psychologically simple.

The operation commenced on the night of 6/7 November with 5 Brigade advancing on the right of the axis of advance and 19 Brigade on the left flank. The two advancing brigades captured Bhimber Gali. Next to be captured by the Rajauri Column was Ramgarh Fort. These were the first features to fall to the advancing troops. The Pakistani defenders reacted violently to the attacks and then consolidated on a massive feature called Pir Badesar that dominated the Column's axis of advance.

268 Infantry Brigade carried out an attack operation named Operation Ranjit to capture this feature. It was a tactically strong locality that overlooked the Seri Valley and protected Jhangar from the north. Deployment on the feature posed a direct threat to Kotli. It also threatened one flank of the line of

communication, near Chingas. Pir Badesar was captured, and Lieutenant Colonel Dharam Singh, CO of 1 Kumaon (Para), was awarded the Mahavir Chakra during the operation.

19 Infantry Brigade came across some determined opposition at Point 5372, a feature located south-east of Mendhar, which guarded the route to Kotli. Continuing to demonstrate against Point 5372 as a ruse, the dominant force switched to the right flank where opposition was light.

These two brigades then captured Pt 5982 and Topa Ridge that lay to the south of Poonch. To achieve the vital link-up, on 20 November, the Poonch Garrison broke through the southern part of their year-long encirclement and traversed the neighbouring hills. On 23 November, Mendhar was captured in a pincer move by 19 Infantry Brigade from the south permitting the Engineers to construct a jeep track via Mendhar to Poonch.

In addition to achieving the vital link-up with the Poonch Garrison, the operation resulted in the capture of 2100 square km of territory. A large number of refugees, including over 10,000 Muslims, were able to escape the wrath of the cruel raiders and obtain some relief from the J&K State Administration.

Although Poonch was linked-up and secured, costly gains made by the Indian 161 Infantry Brigade and 77 Parachute Brigade in the Uri sector were lost. It happened due to the ill-advised vacation of Led Gali and Pir Kanthi picquets in the Haji Pir region for the winter months. This faulty action to escape the winter's cold also allowed Pakistan to occupy these picquets and a large salient centred on the Haji Pir Pass.

Before any action could be taken to recapture the salient, a ceasefire was declared from 2 January 1949, leaving these locations securely in Pakistani hands. Thus, Poonch continues to be a border outpost on the Line of Control (LC) in between the Indian and Pakistani held regions of Jammu & Kashmir.

The decision to relieve and hold Poonch saved thousands of civilian lives but at the military cost of diverting troops from the capture of Domel and Muzzafarabad during a period of vulnerability, as well as diverting troops for the capture of Mirpur and Bhimber.

The saving of Poonch was a more meaningful strategical gambit in 1948, and the areas of Domel and Muzzafarabad are still illegally held by Pakistan.

The Bitter End

[Details of this chapter have been taken from research done by Lieutenant General Harwant Singh (Retd)]

The personality of the general is indispensable. He is the head, he is the all of an army. The Gaul's were not conquered by Roman Legions but by Caesar. It was not before the Carthaginian soldier that Rome was made to tremble, but before Hannibal. It was not the Macedonian phalanx which penetrated India but Alexander. Prussia was not defended for seven years against the three most formidable European powers by Prussian soldiers but by Frederick the Great.

—Napolean

With an intense and single-minded devotion, Pritam kept beating back the raiders and the Pakistan Army to save the Poonch area for India. It is most unfortunate that his many petty-minded detractors failed to appreciate the enormous amount of good work he did for the Indian Army and the country. Blinded by their grudges, these petty individuals were busy collecting evidence to see that he was maligned and betrayed. A considerable amount of professional jealousy existed against Pritam due to his incredible achievements as a soldier. With the great advantage of hindsight, today it is possible to dispassionately view the merits and demerits of the murky events as they unfolded more than seventy years ago.

After the link-up of the forces, the raiders and their Pakistani handlers were pushed westwards, and soon the guns fell silent. Poonch was safe, and the people rejoiced. As has always been the case, once the guns fell silent and dangers receded, the lesser mortals began a sordid, vilification campaign against the harbinger of victory. The role of Brigadier Pritam Singh, MC, in the string of great victories that had saved Srinagar, Poonch, and other areas in Kashmir was quickly forgotten. There was a concerted campaign to tarnish the image of the patriot and hero who had been solely responsible for many spectacular victories.

At a different level, the fate of Poonch still hung in the balance. At the Defence Committee meeting on 3 December 1947, Pandit Nehru had stated that Poonch must be defended at all costs. Mountbatten, however, had a different view at that time. The C-in-C, in his turn, wanted the final orders on Poonch to await the recommendations of Lieutenant General Russell, the Army Commander. Due to tactical and logistic compulsions, General Russell wanted to pull out of Poonch. He had his reservations and thought that a lot of good luck would be required to hold on to Poonch. He never anticipated that the bravery and patriotism of one great soldier—Pritam—would chase off the raiders and hold Poonch for India.

Major General Atma Singh now started subverting the loyalty of Pritam's officers, and at the same time, he began building cases against him. In a letter dated 19 August 1948, Atma informed HQ Western Command that Lieutenant

Colonel Palit (ex-CO 3/9 GR) had told an officer named Colonel Sathe of IA Division that Pritam had shot a Hindu porter, and made his Brigade Major (BM) shoot some Muslim prisoners. He added, "… in case this is true … Pritam must be held guilty of murder and charged accordingly." Atma's lack of fairness and hostility towards Pritam can be judged from this letter alone. He did not carry out any prior investigation before he hurried to inform the Command HQ. Many officers were keen to see Pritam disgraced and punished for reasons of jealousy. These officers cashed in on Atma's animosity towards Pritam. They kept on obliquely filing false reports and goading the Division Commander to take firm action against Pritam.

As differences between Atma and Pritam reached their nadir, the harassed Brigade Commander was forced to complain to his Army Commander. The latter decided to move Pritam to the Kashmir valley in exchange of one Brigadier Dathania. It is quite clear that the higher HQ was keen to use Pritam's battle expertise by sending him to the Kashmir Valley, where operations were still in full swing to oust the raiders. Had HQ decided to send Pritam out of J&K, to any other station in India, history would have turned out very differently. Pritam would not have suffered the ignominy and disgrace ultimately heaped on him. In any case, reactions of the Sri Div (Srinagar Division) Commander, Major General KS Thimayya, DSO, were very pertinent to the situation. Thimayya was getting an excellent soldier, and he warmly welcomed the move to transfer Pritam to the Kashmir Valley, where he would be an asset. But Thimayya warned the Army Commander that if after Pritam's move a disaster befell Poonch, then he would not like to be associated with it. Thereafter, nothing more was ever heard regarding the proposal to move Pritam out of Poonch.

All this while, the enemy had been regularly attacking Poonch with increasing vigour. But nothing could break the resolve of the defenders led by Pritam. The courageous fight continued every day. By this time, the Army Commander had realised that Pritam was doing a tremendous job of saving Poonch and its surrounding areas. He specifically told Atma to "go easy" on Pritam.

Consequently, during the final link-up with Poonch, in November 1948, Atma told Pritam that he had been misinformed about matters in Poonch. He wanted Pritam to forget about all the unpleasantness that had taken place between them. Realising that his superior officer, the Army Commander, had been speaking well of Pritam, during the celebrations of the link-up in the Officers Mess of HQ 19 Infantry Brigade at Rajouri, Atma announced to Pritam, "You have done a very fine job, and I am going to recommend you for the highest gallantry award." This was said in the presence of many other officers. Yet, behind his back, Atma renewed his efforts to build more cases against Pritam!

Meanwhile, at HQ Western Command, the campaign of vilification came to a head. An enquiry was ordered into the charges and counter-charges levelled between Atma and Pritam. Within a few days, both officers were called to Delhi by the C-in-C, General Cariappa. The C-in-C acknowledged that Pritam had creditably accomplished a very tough and professionally sound task at Poonch. He assured Pritam that all would be well, and specially told Atma that the entire ongoing case should be closed. Pritam left Delhi feeling relieved that the C-in-C had in no uncertain terms told Atma to stop troubling him. He felt grateful that he could now concentrate on removing the last of the remaining enemy forces holding out on the heights surrounding Poonch.

However, Pritam was in for a rude shock some days later when Army HQ ordered a Court of Inquiry (COI) to investigate the case. Major General Khanolkar was appointed as the Presiding Officer and Brigadier BM Kaul as one of its members. As the C-in-C, General Cariappa was a very senior functionary in the new government at Delhi. So it is inevitable that pressures from the highest levels must have come into play to make the C-in-C do a volte-face and order the COI. The action was quite uncharacteristic of General Cariappa, who was known for his values of fairplay and righteousness. It was shocking because the COI was ordered after assuring Pritam that all would be well, and telling Major General Atma Singh not to harass his Brigade Commander.

The COI, that should have been a fair and impartial exercise, distinguished itself by a visible bias against Pritam. There was unseemly prejudice, partisan behaviour, breach of procedures and blatant violation of the norms and canons of natural justice. Very strangely, and quite contrary to existing rules, the Court would not allow Pritam to cross-examine any of the witnesses. Members of COI would record evidence in their own words, rather than recording the exact words of the witnesses. Norms were violated when recorded statements were not read out to Pritam, for his knowledge of what a witness had stated. Justice stood blatantly subverted for the accused did not know what had been recorded by the Court!

At one stage, the Court went from Meerut to Dehra Dun to record the statement of the Rajah of Poonch, who was an important prosecution witness. However, they did not take Pritam along, and the Rajah recorded his statement behind Pritam's back. Once again, it was in total contravention of the Army rules. If a witness said anything that went in favour of Pritam, the Court threatened him. It appeared as if the Court had been secretly briefed to conduct its proceedings against Pritam, and the members would often shout to try and browbeat him.

In another incidence of a procedural violation, the Court went to Poonch and took with it Major General Atma Singh,

Mr Raina (political advisor to Sheikh Abdullah), the ex-Wazir of Poonch, and Lieutenant Colonel Dharam Singh, but did not take along Pritam. From Poonch, two members of the Court, along with Atma Singh and Raina, went to Srinagar in a RIAF aircraft demanded for the purpose. No one seems to know who they discussed matters with at Srinagar. Pritam appealed against the Court travelling to Poonch without him but to no avail.

It is worth recalling the irony of the drama that would take place whenever the Court met. The person most often guilty of displaying his temper, browbeating, shouting, threatening and thumping the table at Pritam, was a member of the COI named Brigadier (later Lieutenant General) BM (Bijji) Kaul. It was a well-known fact that Bijji Kaul was close to Pandit Jawaharlal Nehru, the Prime Minister. Some eleven years later, in 1962, this officer, as the Corps Commander in NEFA, was to suffer disgrace for the Army and the country by proving to be thoroughly incompetent.

Lieutenant General BM (Bijji) Kaul

Predictably, the findings and opinion of the COI led to the slapping of 26 charges against Pritam. Eighteen out of these were for abetment to the commissioning of murder by the BM Major Pran Nath. One charge was for abetment of theft of a carpet (12ft x 12ft) by Subedar Major Sher Singh. Another two charges were for criminal breach of trust regarding public funds, and three charges were for voluntarily causing hurt to three J&K Police personnel.

At the Summary of Evidence (S of E), the prosecution case on the preposterous charges of abetment of murders could not stand scrutiny. On Pritam's attitude towards Muslims, the defence produced evidence to establish that before his arrival, some Muslims had been killed in the township. However, within a few days of Pritam taking over as the Garrison Commander of Poonch, Muslims could freely move around in the town. Suleiman, an electrician, was attacked by refugees and Pritam himself had rushed forward to rescue him. From time to time, Muslim prisoners were released to proceed to the territory held by Pakistan, and often Pritam gave them money from his pocket, as they were leaving. Lieutenant Colonel Chandar Singh deposed to the effect that on one occasion, Pritam had borrowed Rs 25 from him, to give to the released prisoners.

Some police personnel, while escorting prisoners up to the border, had let the refugees kill them. When he heard of this incident, Pritam immediately went to the site and brought back the only surviving prisoner, who was severely wounded and had been found hiding in the bushes. Pritam had him admitted to the hospital for treatment. That is where he gave the taste of the rough end of his stick to the concerned police personnel. Pakistan had complained to India about the ill-treatment of Muslims by the Indian troops in other sectors, but none against those at Poonch.

Lieutenant Colonel Bakshish Singh, one of the company commanders at Poonch during the siege, and a veteran of many battles of World War II had this to say about the treatment of prisoners by Pritam, "... from time to time prisoners were released because there was no food to spare in those days. Pritam was too brave a man to order his troops to carry out the cowardly act of shooting prisoners. He was more favourably inclined towards Muslims than Hindus and Sikhs because the Muslims were the underdogs at Poonch." While the charges of abetment to murder had no chance of sticking, they had propaganda value and showed the extent to which Pritam's detractors were out to get at him.

The charge of the alleged theft of a carpet became most infamous. The story went something like this. In May 1948, a carpet was to be sent from Poonch to Jammu for onward dispatch to the RIAF at Palam and was temporarily placed with the heavy baggage of 1 Kumaon (Para). On 5 July 1948, Pritam had this carpet placed with the Air Transport Unit at the Poonch airfield. He further instructed that it be handed over to Major MS Grewal, Air Liaison Transport Officer (ALTO), who would send it to Palam for handing it over to the Air Force. It was a present from the Rajah of Poonch.

On 9 July 1948, Subedar Major Sher Singh was brought before Major General Atma Singh in connection with items from the Poonch palace found in his baggage during the search at Poonch airfield. Besides other complaints against Pritam, he also made a mention of this carpet to him.

Sub Maj Sher Singh

Consequently, an enquiry regarding the carpet was conducted on 16 July 1948, by a Major Joshi. On 28 July, the carpet was seized on orders of Atma and placed at Jammu. Brigadier Pritam protested against this and took up the issue.

At the Court Martial, the Prosecution's case was that Pritam was not interested in presenting the carpet to the RIAF, but wanted to take the said carpet for himself. The Subedar Major produced a memo dated 3 July 1948, signed by him, Hon. Lieutenant Rai, Head Clerk of 1 Kumaon (Para) and some others, stating that a carpet measuring 14'9" x 14'9" had been handed over to Brigadier Pritam Singh in their presence. For purposes of identification at a later date, a portion of the border—*jhallar*—was cut and a gash made in one corner of the carpet. During cross-examination, it transpired that the prosecution witnesses had made no mention of this memo, the cutting of the *jhallar* or the gash during the inquiry held by Major Joshi, or at the Court of Inquiry (COI).

Major MS Grewal, ALTO, deposed that Pritam had instructed him in July 1948 that the carpet deposited with the Air Maintenance Unit at Jammu, was to be sent to Palam for delivery to the RIAF. Further, RIAF aircraft flying records brought out that from 5 July to 28 July 1948, no RIAF aircraft flew from Jammu to Palam airport. The Prosecution's case regarding the alleged theft of a carpet by Brigadier Pritam Singh was thus hopelessly flawed. There was ample reason to believe that a forged document and false evidence had been surreptitiously introduced by motivated members of the Court to provide false evidence against Pritam and further malign the accused.

The last two charges pertained to defrauding public funds from the Imprest Account in two claims. Pritam was accused of defrauding Rs 13,182 and 8 annas in one case and Rs 2,603 and 2 annas in another case. The Prosecution claimed that the amounts mentioned above were more than the actual expenditure on local purchase of firewood, rations, etc. The Prosecution contended that Pritam wanted to keep to himself the excess amount of Rs 10,062 and 9 annas. It alleged that when Lieutenant Colonel Dharam Singh was appointed as the

Commanding Officer (CO) of 1 Kumaon (Para) with effect from 6 December 1947, he was only responsible for "operations", while Brigadier Pritam Singh, the Brigade Commander, was responsible for administration, discipline and other such related duties. Therefore, Lieutenant Colonel Dharam Singh claimed that he did not know that these claims were false.

The Prosecution's case rested on Brigade Routine Order (BRO) No. 104 dated 13 March 1948, wherein it was stated that Lieutenant Colonel Dharam Singh would be the operational commander and that Brigadier Pritam Singh would attend to matters of administration, discipline, etc. Thereby, the Quarter Master (QM), Major Sukhdarshan Singh, had dealt with Pritam on the issue of these claims, without the knowledge of Lieutenant Colonel Dharam Singh, CO. Further, on 23 July 1948, Sukhdarshan said he gave the surplus amount of about Rs 10,062 to Pritam. Subedar Major Sher Singh deposed that Brigadier Pritam Singh gave him this amount on 27 July 1948 for safe-keeping in the treasury chest of the unit, saying that it was his money.

The Defence case was that BRO No. 104 was published after the Khanetar Ridge fiasco, where Dharam and his Adjutant had thrown their weapons in the face of the enemy and run away from the action leaving behind many dead, wounded and heavy weapons. This incident had lowered the morale of the unit, and it was felt that the continued direct association of Pritam with the unit needed to be shown to the troops. There was no change in the "command and control" of the battalion. In any case, this BRO No. 104 was published on 13 January whereas the claims for local purchase were made on 24 January and 28 January. Further, during this period, Dharam, on his admission, had conducted some Summary CourtMartial trials and initiated confidential reports of his officers. It is a well-known fact that only a commanding officer with full administrative and disciplinary powers can hold a Summary Court Martial and initiate confidential reports on his officers.

The Defence also produced another BRO on 24 April 1948, which read, "Hereafter all matters pertaining to the battalion be referred to Lieutenant Colonel Dharam Singh". It explained the rationale of the earlier BRO because this second BRO was published after the Khanetar Ridge was recaptured. It was also brought out that the two contingent bills for about Rs 13,182 and Rs 2,603 were signed on 24 and 28 January 1948, by Lieutenant Colonel Dharam Singh along with the three obligatory certificates on each, as to their authenticity and truthfulness, in capacity of CO, 1 Kumaon (Para). HQ Western Command then countersigned these Contingent Bills. At that time Pritam was only the Imprest Account holder of Poonch, and he had signed the monthly account of the sum of money received and expended by all units at Poonch. The responsibility for the correctness of individual contingent bills was that of the respective commanding officers and the counter-signing authority.

Major Sukhdarshan Singh, who was the Second-in-Command (2IC) of 1 Kumaon (Para), deposed before the Court in June 1948 that in his presence, Dharam had informed Pritam that about Rs 10,000 was rendered surplus in local purchases and wanted to credit the same to the battalion's private funds. To this, Pritam had told him that he would obtain necessary orders from the GOC. Thus, the 2IC's subsequent statement that he handed over about Rs 10,000 to Pritam in his office on 23 July 1948 appears to be flawed. It should be seen in the light of the fact that Pritam was wounded on 21 July 1948, and confined to bed for two weeks. Under no circumstances could he have been in his office to receive the said cash, nor could he have handed over this money to the Subedar Major on 27 July, when there was a treasury chest in the Brigade HQ itself.

Several witnesses, including Major General Kalwant Singh, who was General Officer Commanding (GOC) of Jammu IA Division during the period under reference, had visited Poonch five to six times. Kalwant deposed that Dharam was the CO of the Battalion in every respect. On the Prosecution's plea and Dharam's deposition that he was not the CO, Sardar Swaran Singh, Defence Counsel and later India's Minister of External Affairs, made the most pointed observation at Pritam's court-martial. While addressing the Court, he said, "If Lieutenant Colonel Dharam Singh was not the CO, then how could he have dealt with disciplinary cases? He admits having tried men of his unit by Summary Court Martial (SCM). He now wishes you to believe that he used to consult the accused (Pritam) before disposing of the cases. In an SCM, the CO constitutes the Court, and it is he who takes the oath. If this is what the witness had been doing, then my submission is that the witness is not worthy of any credit. Besides being a liar, he is utterly dishonest."

Poonch continued to be under siege all this while with ever-increasing pressure from the enemy. Pritam was mounting, on an average, one operation a week to capture the surrounding heights and raid areas for collection of food grains for the population. He raised and trained two battalions from the people of Poonch and administered the Brigade, which comprised a large number of units. With these commitments at hand, it is very doubtful if he would have had the time or inclination to go into the internal administration of 1 Kumaon (Para). It appears all the more relevant, when his association with the unit was of only two months, whereas Dharam had been with the unit for six years.

Then there was the letter introduced by the Prosecution—from Lieutenant Colonel Dharam Singh to IA Division, dated 16 July 1948, reporting the theft of a carpet and defrauding of public funds by Brigadier Pritam Singh. Surprisingly, on its receipt by IA Division, this letter bore no stamp of the Division or initials of any officer. Both these actions were mandatory on the part of the formation's office whenever they received a document. The AO stated that he never saw this letter at Jammu Division. Thus, the letter appeared to have been introduced later as an after-thought, and it was perhaps intelligently forged.

The Prosecution case against Pritam of defrauding public funds had no merit. Instead, it was Lieutenant Colonel Dharam Singh who stood indicted for defrauding in the instant case, and on his admission, in the case of four other claims amounting to about Rs 11,423 preferred by him in June 1948. Yet, the Court returned a verdict of guilty on this charge against Brigadier Pritam Singh, MC!

Lieutenant General Harwant Singh, the former Deputy Chief of Army Staff, recalls having regular meetings with Sardar Swaran Singh in the early nineties. He asked Swaran Singh how a court composed of such experienced officers accepted a patently absurd contention of the Prosecution that Lieutenant Colonel Dharam Singh was only an "operational CO", to the total exclusion of administration and such other duties, in the face of clinching evidence to the contrary, and return a verdict of guilty.

Sardar Swaran Singh could not recall all the details after a lapse of nearly forty-three years but remembered Pritam as an honourable and courageous man. He maintained there was no case against Pritam. His conviction was political vendetta, where Sheikh Abdullah and others had used their clout at Delhi to obtain a verdict of guilty.

General Harwant Singh also asked Major General Niranjan Prasad, a contemporary of Pritam, as to how Major General JN Chaudhary—the Presiding Officer—had accepted the impossible stand of the Prosecution. The latter observed, "Over-ambition can destroy a conscience."

Major General Virendra Singh, another contemporary of Pritam, said, "It was Bijjee Kaul (BM Kaul) who was working overtime, along with others in Delhi, to hunt down Pritam".

In *The Times of India* dated 15 May 2018, Lieutenant General HS Panag, a former Northern Army Commander wrote an article titled *A Hero Disowned by the Nation Deserves Pardon.* To quote him verbatim:

> The end of the war brought up another phenomenon—jealousy and intrigues among the senior officers most of whom had been catapulted to higher ranks without command of units and some without spending a single day in battle. The larger-than-life, mercurial Brigadier Pritam Singh was ensnared in this web of deceit.

However, there are hints of a much broader conspiracy, aimed at Kalwant Singh and Baba Mehar Singh, in the late Major General Sukhwant Singh's book *India's* Wars *Since Independence* (Lancer Publishers, 2009):

> The end of the little war brought up another phenomenon—character assassination. Petty jealousies surfaced among the general officers and intrigues flourished, leading to the trial by court-martial of Pritam Singh, the hero of Poonch, for alleged connivance in the theft of two carpets from the local palace. Although Pritam Singh was ostensibly on trial, **the conspirators were bent on implicating Kalwant Singh and Mehar Singh** [emphasis added].
>
> It is said that Thimayya, a defence witness, stated "... without Pritam, there would have been no Poonch, and with Poonch would have gone these carpets. Why are you crucifying this good soldier for nothing?" Pritam Singh was unceremoniously dismissed from service. Kalwant Singh was subsequently superseded by some of the generals involved in the plot who had not even heard a shot fired in anger. Baba Mehar Singh, by then a legendary figure in

> the services, resigned in disgust to become the personal pilot of a dethroned maharaja and this was to have serious repercussions later.

In another chapter of the same book—*The Military Leadership*—he writes:

> General Kalwant Singh organised the Jammu and Kashmir operational theatre from scratch with no, or minimal, infrastructure and conducted operations there with such great energy and dispatch that the Pakistani raiders were hurled back from sensitive areas. He set the theatre on such firm footing that its transformation later into a corps zone was easy. Yet, when his turn for promotion came, he was passed over by juniors who had nothing to show except some "sergeant majoring" in otherwise peaceful cantonments.
>
> Another case in point is that of Brigadier Pritam Singh, commonly known as and virtually worshipped by the local populace as the saviour of Poonch. That indomitable spirit defied its capture against heavy odds with a surrounded garrison with minimal resources. Even for food, he had to raid Pakistani-held territory to harvest grain. Instead of being honoured by the nation, he was court-martialled on a trivial charge of theft of a carpet from the Poonch palace.
>
> Baba Mehar Singh, the best combat pilot of his times, enterprisingly used Dakotas as bombers, flew the first aircraft to Leh, and supplied the Poonch garrison under fire at night without adequate navigational aids. He personally led each mission and won the esteem of the ground force. In fact, his name became a legend, yet he had to resign his commission under unpalatable pressures.
>
> In short, it appears there has been a deliberate attempt to destroy the image of crisis leadership ... Ironically, achievement

> in the field became a hurdle in promoting one's military career, infighting and jealousy among generals may have strengthened the politician's hands, but this was a grave injustice to posterity. It was amply evidenced in the debacle at Thagla when the Chinese struck in 1962. Non-entities like Niranjan Prasad, Umrao Singh and (Bijjee) Kaul, brought to the fore by our inept systems, compounded an ineffaceable humiliation for the nation. Nehru died trying to live it down.

Within the Service, Pritam had not only superseded quite a few colleagues but had emerged as a great military leader, to the envy of many others. Outside the Service circles, the vengeful animosity against Pritam was born out of a propaganda blitz and disinformation campaign mounted by certain politically influential people in J&K State. False and inaccurate information was spread to demonise Pritam. This information included reports of the levelling of an old graveyard to prepare the landing strip at Poonch, false propaganda regarding shooting of Muslim prisoners, rude treatment meted out to Sheikh Abdullah and his companions by the refugees at Poonch, Wazir's removal and making him part with a gold-threaded Choga and diamond-studded sword and other concocted tales. These were some of the contributory factors for the animus against Pritam.

It is claimed that Major General Atma Singh even produced two Muslim women from Poonch before Bakhshi Ghulam Mohd, at Jammu. During the siege of Poonch, these two women were accosted by the police for some nefarious activities in connivance with a National Conference worker, who escaped before he could be arrested. These women were instructed to tell Bakhshi that Pritam assaulted them.

The C-in-C approved the verdict of "guilty" for the charge of fraud. But he did not approve the verdict of "not guilty" for the charge of theft of a carpet. The theft of carpets (not just a carpet) had been publicised so much that a verdict of "not guilty" would have become extremely embarrassing for Pritam's detractors. It would have exposed the mendacious nature of their charges.

After the Kashmir War, the opposing commanders met frequently. Referring to these meetings, General KS Thimayya, DSO, stated, "I do not remember them (Pakistani officers) ever complaining (of ill-treatment of prisoners) against Pritam. In fact, on my first meeting, late Brigadier Sher Khan mentioned that if he admired anybody at all on the Indian side, it was Pritam, who had fought most gallantly against our overwhelming forces around Poonch."

Today very few know of this great son of India. But to the people of Poonch and especially for those 40,000 refugees and their descendants, he is a saviour. Even today, Pritam's faded and yellowing photographs adorn many homes in Poonch. Those who lived through that year-long ordeal and had a glimpse of the iron in his soul, his great resolve, courage and unwavering love for India, hold him in great reverence.

Sadly, the Court-Martial deprived Pritam of his Service career, and even his "Independence Medal". What they could not take away from him was the Military Cross and the medals he had won during World War II, while operating under orders of the British. The detractors not only maligned and sullied Pritam's reputation but also buried the great story of the year-long heroic siege of Poonch. It was a complete sacrilege, as the year-long siege had been unique in itself and worthy to rank amongst the great sieges in the history of warfare. If the story had not been buried, it would have become a subject of study in military institutions all over the world.

Nations that treat their heroes in this shabby manner do not produce them in great numbers.

Therefore, some eleven years later, when the Chinese came to push us down from the Himalayan heights from Kibbutho (NEFA) in the east to the Karakoram in the west, the Indian Army could not field a single Pritam Singh who could arrest the invading forces. Many brave officers and men who despised yielding ground to the swarming enemy and tried upholding national and military honour, went down fighting at their distant posts. However, they did so in vain! They vainly looked for a commander who could rally them and give no quarter to the enemy, one who would stand and fight, rather than tamely suffer the ignominy of a general rout. With its badly bruised ego and lost pride, the nation could not throw up a military leader with resolve and defiance to stand up to the Chinese in that moment of national crisis—stand up for just a few weeks—as India's greatest ally, the Himalayan winter was already menacingly closing in on the enemy. In this hour of need, a man like Pritam was sorely required to replicate the gallant stand that he had taken at Shalateng and Poonch! A man like Pritam was desperately needed to redeem our national pride.

Pritam's appeal for justice and equity to his Chief was of no avail. Here was a man, who had always stood by the Tricolour and braved the great storms which raged in Kashmir and Poonch. Sadly, now in this hour of a personal crisis, he had no one to stand for him—neither his Chief, nor the media, nor any public-spirited men.

Here then was a man, whom the might of Pakistan Army in its year-long endeavour could not pull down, but was finally felled by his people!

When Pritam had been hounded for two long years, stripped of his rank, unfairly called a murderer, a sadist, a thief and a cheat, he wrote: "Sometimes serious doubts assail me whether it would have been better to have let the State Forces garrison slip out of Poonch and merely follow them, than to have put up that tenacious fight, but I dispel them with my conviction that I have done my duty to India and I know that one day the truth will come out".

Monty Palit's Testimony

Excerpts from Musings and *Memories Volume 1*, Major General DK Palit, VrC (Palit & Palit in association with Lancer Publishers, 2004)

Pages 248-253:

The Kashmir war had just broken out and Poonch had been isolated and in dire need of reinforcement. We were ordered to fly into Jammu in aircraft of the National Airways, and thence to Poonch in Air Force Dakotas. We nine Indians—Self, Pesi Dhanbura Second-in-Command, Harry FitzGerald, "Bunny" Malhotra, "Baba" Cariappa, "Krish" Krishnamurthy, an ex-Ordnance officer called Doss and Om Malhotra—had been in command just over a fortnight. A daunting task!

Cariappa's "A" company was the first to be airlifted to Poonch—and then the weather broke. The rest of us were held up in Jammu for two weeks. On the fourth or fifth day the GOC,

General Kulwant Singh, sent for me. When I walked into his office, he threw a piece of paper down on the desk in front of me.

"Read that, Palit!"

It was a signal from Local Brigadier Pritam Singh, Officiating Brigade Commander of Poonch Brigade.

It read:

"3/9 GR unbattleworthy. Request their removal and replacement by Indian troops."

The world seemed to collapse around me. Not only the shame; there was also the fear of losing my command. But Kulwant was an understanding man.

"Palit, if you had been in command six months, I would have sacked you on the spot. But I know you are new in the unit. Now, fly into Poonch tomorrow—soggy airfield or not—and sort out your Battalion. I'll give you three months, then if your unit is still unbattleworthy—you'll be for the sack."

I was flown in with my orderly in a Harvard aircraft the very next day.

Poonch was the seat of the Raja of a collateral tributary state under the Maharaja of Kashmir. It was located in a deep valley set in a nexus of mountain ranges to the east of the Jhelum (after its southward turn from Muzaffarabad). Unlike the docile and friendly Kashmiri Muslims, the people of Poonch were the warlike Sudhans, people who had originated from the Black Mountain area of Hazara—and were fanatically anti-Dogra. They were freely recruited in the Indian Army and, therefore, militarily trained. It was they who now surrounded Poonch town, where 35,000 or so Sikh and Dogra refugees from western Kashmir had taken shelter. They were hoping to starve the refugees into submission followed by wholesale massacre, as had happened at Mirpur and Kotli, townships further west.

Pritam Singh met me on the airstrip. A tall Sikh of military bearing, he was about two years my senior (though, being an ex-ranker commission, many years older). The reason why he was in command of the Brigade was that none of the senior Sandhurst-commissioned officers would agree to take over the beleaguered garrison of Poonch!

"Well, Palit," he said, after our mutual greetings had been formally made, "The GOC may have given you three months, but I can't. I don't have the time. I'll give you just two weeks—to get your Battalion into operational shape. At the moment, to judge from your "A" Company here, they are a bunch of undisciplined rabble—and cowards to boot. Two weeks Palit, then if you haven't delivered—out you go, both you and your men."

I spoke to Baba Cariappa when I moved into our Camp. He said that during a joint attack with a company of Kumaonis (who were the only other Indian troops in Poonch, besides three "refugee" battalions of Kashmir State Forces) his men had lain down on the ground and refused to advance when ordered! Only Cariappa and one Gorkha OR, his orderly, had gone into the attack.

I promoted that lone GOR to Lance Naik and put him up for an IDSM award, and I sent the GO of the Company, Jemadar Lall Bahadur, off to Brigade HQ with a request that he be repatriated to India on the first flight that came in from Jammu. (My rejects seemed to have made a habit of coming back and making good. Lall Bahadur was sent back from the Centre and ended the Siege of Poonch with a Mahavir Chakra and bar).

There was a spell of good weather then and soon the old fleet of Dakota workhorses brought in the remainder of my Battalion (though with only light weaponry and equipment, as yet).

3/9 GR had been allotted Sheesh Mahal for its accommodation, a small double-storied walled-in building about half a mile to the south of the Raja's Palace, Moti Mahal, newly occupied by Brigade HQ and personnel of 1st Kumaon not deployed on the heights surrounding Poonch. (The Raja and his cousin, the owner of Sheesh

Mahal, had been evacuated to Dehra Dun). After the greater part of one rifle company was sent up to occupy new piquets on the surrounding peaks—or to relieve some Kumaoni-held piquets—the rest of the Battalion fitted into Sheesh Mahal and its walled compound. The terraced fields outside, gradually sloping down to the Batar Nullah, provided adequate training ground.

I suspected that the anti-Indian propaganda spread by the departing British officers was the root cause of the low morale of the men. Fortunately, the CO of the 1st Kashmir (SF) Battalion was a very senior Lieutenant Colonel called Hira Nand Dubey, whose younger brother in the Indian Army, Uday Dubey (Sandhurst commission) I had known quite well in Delhi. I went to HND to seek his advice on how to handle the situation.

Hira was quite definite with his advice: "Ask the Brigade Commander to send your whole Battalion out on an operation. Get them blooded under the command of Indians. Don't waste your time on drill, weapon-training or any such activity. They are an organised unit—all they now need is confidence in their officers."

I think that was the wisest and most important advice anyone ever gave me during my whole career in the Army.

Pritam readily agreed. There was a ready-made task I could carry out, he said.

The garrison of Poonch had till then been confined to the east bank of the Batar River. There were not enough troops to expand the defensive perimeter to include the west bank, from where we were constantly shelled or mortared. The task Pritam allotted me was to capture the long, low ridge that ran north-south, about two furlongs back from the banks of the Batar.

After dark, a couple of nights later, we crossed the Batar at a ford a little upstream from Sheesh Mahal, carrying only small arms and platoon mortars (I don't think the three-inchers had arrived by then). We had to make the attack under our own steam, so to say—no covering fire.

We crept up the track towards the ridge, whatever clanking noises we made cloaked by the murmur of the fast-flowing Batar. My plan was to attack the centre-point of the ridge (we had made a recce with our field glasses from Poonch) with three companies up, each under command of an Indian officer. The reserve company would be commanded by a Gurkha officer—our old friend ex-SM Man Bahadur, now returned to us from the Centre, as a Direct Commissioned Captain. After reaching the crest, the two flank companies would turn right and left and move north and south along the ridge, clearing any enemy who might still be holding out.

I kept the front line bunched together in the dark, visibility being limited to a star-lit range of sight. I couldn't risk loss of control—in case the men turned and ran!

Well, they didn't run: but they did the next best thing—they went to ground, *a la* Cariappa's experience.

Just as we had negotiated the lower, gentler slopes and began to climb, there were a few shots from up above us—fired at random in our direction, it being too dark to take aim. And the whole lot in front of me went down like an alley of ninepins!

I shouted abuse at them, hit them on their arses with my walking stick—to no avail. I heard Man Bahadur come up behind me and he belaboured them even more vigorously—and abused them in much more choice terms than I had done (my first lesson in Gorkhali!)

I couldn't see to the left and right beyond the limited starlit range but I could hear Bunny's choice Punjabi vocabulary, not keeping his voice down either. I learned new words from him too!

"Get in front and drag the b———s up," I yelled at him into the dark. Man Bahadur had begun to do that already.

It took time but at last the advance resumed. More firing: no reaction. As we neared the crest, I shouted out to the flank commanders NOT to fix bayonets—never a clever thing to do in the dark. "Go in firing," I yelled.

They did, and routed the few enemy troops on the crest.

We never looked back, after that night. We fought throughout the war, lost hundreds in dead or wounded—officers, GOs, men—and even the CO sent back to hospital to recover from wounds; but they never again faltered. (Details of this battle are given on pages 271 to 278).

Pages 255–280:

Pritam Singh and the Defence of Poonch 1947–48

No senior field commander in the Indian Army has displayed as much steadfastness, resolution, physical and moral courage in battle as Pritam Singh of the 4th/19th Hyderabadis (now The Kumaon Regiment). In that first war against Pakistan, his leadership—not only of the troops he commanded but also of the inhabitants trapped in that besieged enclave, he shone forth like a beacon. He emerged as the greatest hero of that war, but whereas others of his ilk were awarded DSOs and OBEs or their Indian counterparts, Pritam ended up by being court-martialled and hounded out of the Army in disgrace—caught in the crossfire of a couple of in-fighting Generals.

I served with Pritam in Poonch; and I have no hesitation in recording that in the perilous and near-hopeless situation that prevailed in that enemy-surrounded portion of India, Pritam was a source of morale and motivation for all of us. He combined the earthy pragmatism of the ex-ranker with sensitivity uncommon in men with backgrounds rooted in the soil—qualities that, in addition to his courage and leadership, made him virtually an object of worship by the many thousands of inhabitants of Poonch throughout the war. And he has remained installed in the altars of their hearts till this day: witness the Pritam Singh Satsang of Poonch, started and kept in being by people who still worship his memory.

In trying to defend his name and repute, I myself nearly had to leave the Army; and I probably would have, had I not been hastily sent out of the country when the proceedings against Pritam were initiated, with the jackals in full cry giving him chase. By the time I returned to India two years later, Pritam had been cashiered and sent home in disgrace. Wars and alarums of war kept me busy; and inevitably the memory of Pritam Singh and the injustice meted out to him faded from the mind.

It was not until many years later, long after I had retired from the Service, that I read in a back copy of the USI Journal, a letter to the editor written by a Brigadier Butalia, pleading that even now, with Pritam long dead, his case be juridically reviewed and a war hero restored to his pedestal.

Butalia's letter stirred my conscience. Pritam had been court-martialed and sentenced while I was out of India, on a posting to Egypt from 1949 to 1951. Although my refusal to give evidence against Pritam on a charge of murder when arm-twisted by GOC-in-C Cariappa in 1948, had resulted in the charge being dropped, Pritam had been tried and sentenced for lesser charges—of embezzlement, defalcation and the looting of *objects d'art* and weapons from Poonch Palace.

(The murder charge that was dropped, related to an incident in the heat of battle when Pritam had shot down a fleeing stretcher-bearer in order to prevent the spread of panic among the troops—a perfectly legitimate, if drastic, solution. But because Pritam had later reported the death as a war casualty, to enable his family to draw a pension, Cariappa had vindictively wanted to depict the case as one of murder).

I decided that even at this late stage I should try to do *something* "to restore justice to his memory"—if not to annul the court-martial's verdict and sentence, at least to alleviate the character-damage done to him and, if possible, obtain a posthumous pardon from the President of India. So I wrote out in brief the saga of Poonch and Pritam's illustrious role in it and obtained the help of a former ADC of mine, now the Director of Military Training—General Ram Naidu—who very kindly offered to dig out and study the records of Pritam's court-martial and prepare a supporting annexure to my account of the campaign.

Now read on.

I start with my letter to the Director of the USI (Major General Samir Sinha) in whose Journal I had read Butalia's letter :

Major General DK Palit, VrC 1/9 Shanti Niketan
New Delhi 110021
2nd June 1995

My dear Samir,

When I read Brigadier Butalia's letters in back copies of your Journal, I suffered a pang of conscience. The Brigadier is quite right: Pritam was one of the most stalwart and staunch commanders in the First Kashmir War. His denigration was the result of intrigue and malice among general officers. I know: I was inadvertently involved in it.

The process of Pritams's persecution, despite his gallant leadership in Poonch, led to his court-martial; and it was the machinations of the GOC (Atma Singh) and the duplicity of the Army Commander (Cariappa) that embroiled me in an intrigue that eventually led to my sending in my resignation from the Army, rather than be forced to give evidence against my Brigade Commander. As it happened, the CGS did not accept my resignation; and I was sent out of the country while Pritam was being hounded out of the Army because of the implacable enmity between two Generals

(Cariappa and Kulwant).

It all happened nearly fifty years ago. All concerned have since died: Atma, in a road accident soon after the event; Kulwant in the late sixties; Pritam some years ago; and Cariappa recently. I am reluctant to say my piece so many decades later because I am sure that it would not be of help. I doubt if even the legal papers of the case would be available today. At the same time, if there is any *formal* move to re-open Pritam's case and grant him a posthumous acquittal and exoneration, my statement would clearly help in the process. I have, therefore, decided to record my story and to send it to you for use in whatever way that might promote Pritam's cause. You might like to send a copy to Butalia, for he seems the most likely person to take up the cudgels on Pritam's behalf. (It is too long to be printed as a contribution to the Journal; nor, in my opinion, entirely suitable). I have served under senior Indian Generals in the field and in peace. No one ever measured up to the immaculate and dauntless leadership of Pritam Singh. What can one do, nearly fifty years after the event, to restore justice to his memory?

Use the "article" in any way you like.

Yours sincerely,
Sd / DKP

Major General Samir Sinha, PVSM
Director, United Services Institute
Kashmir House, Rajaji Marg
New Delhi – 110011

I had never met Pritam Singh before I went to Poonch in December 1947 in command of 3/9 GR. He had left the IMA the term before I joined it in 1937; and during the War our paths had never crossed. The first time I heard his name was in late November 1947, when GOC Jammu and Kashmir Division (JAK Div) Major General Kulwant Singh, called me to his office, a few days after my arrival in Jammu.

Only a fortnight previously I had taken over command of 3/9 Gurkha Rifles in Gurgaon from its old British officers. As I have already mentioned, before then Indian officers had never been allowed to serve in Gurkha regiments, a key factor in Britain's pre-war imperial policy. The taking-over process had not been a happy experience. The British CO (a very gallant soldier, incidentally) and one or two other British officers did everything they could to undermine the standing of incoming Indian officers. They had advised the GOs (JCOs) and men to leave the Army and go home instead of serving on under "corrupt" Indians who would, they said, need to be bribed before they granted promotions. At the same time, the Brits did not exactly establish their own moral integrity when they unashamedly took away much of the Mess silver—either to donate to departing British regiments or even stole some pieces of silver (and other regimental private property) for themselves. The peccancies were brought to my notice by Gurkha NCOs who had held charge over the looted property. Even the CO, I was told by the Mess Havildar, had items of looted Mess crockery and a war trophy from Indonesia, in his tent. However, I did not pursue these allegations, absolving the NCOs concerned of all responsibility in the matter.

A few days later, the Brigade Commander (Lakhinder Singh) called me to his office and showed me a piece of irrefutable evidence that corroborated the British officers' anti-Indian activities. I decided to act at once to move the CO out of the Battalion two weeks before he was due to leave. For outward appearances, I gave him a customary ceremonial, if unemotional, send-off. I also asked him to leave behind the looted regimental property in his tent. Within a few days of that unfortunate episode, the First Kashmir War having begun, I received orders for a fly-in to Poonch, via Jammu.

With that background, my heart sank when the GOC showed me a signal from Lieutenant Colonel (Local Brigadier) Pritam Singh, officiating Commander Poonch Brigade, referring to the company of 3/9 G R that had been flown into Poonch a few days previously (after which the weather had closed in, preventing further induction of the rest of my Battalion). The message from Pritam was forthright and stark:

"3/9 Gurkhas unbattleworthy stop request no further induction and also withdrawal of Gurkhas already here stop request replacement by Indian troops when available."

Kulwant told me that he had ascertained the facts from Pritam. During an offensive operation aimed at extending the perimeter of the hemmed-in and beleaguered garrison of Poonch, the men of "A" Company 3/9 GR had laid down on the hillside when ordered to go into the attack. Only the company commander, Baba Cariappa, and his orderly had advanced into action; the rest of the company refused to budge.

Kulwant ordered me to fly into Poonch at once. He would send in the rest of the Battalion as and when the newly levelled Poonch airstrip could again take Dakotas.

Pritam was at the airport to meet me when we made a hair-raising landing on the postage-stamp-sized airstrip amidst Kashmir State Forces barracks (surrounded by looming hills on three sides). The fair-weather airstrip of minimum dimensions had been laid by flattening out some of the State Forces barracks.

Pritam was in ill humour because Kulwant had insisted on the Gurkhas remaining in Poonch. Like many Indian officers those days, he was suspicious and distrustful of the very name "Gurkha", because of their past potential as a counter-poise against Indian troops in case of another possible uprising like the Great Rebellion of 1857 (when the Gurkhas had taken a leading part in its suppression). When I explained the special circumstances of the change-over from British to Indian command, he relented somewhat.

I will now quote from my book: *J&K Arms: The History of the J&K Rifles:*

> Brigadier Pritam Singh had set about constructing an airstrip in the area of the JAK Force barracks by the Batar Nullah, about a mile west of Poonch Fort. Thousands of refugees volunteered to work with the troops—and in just over a fortnight, on 12 December, Air Vice Marshal Mukherjee (subsequently Chief of Air Staff) and Air Commodore Mehr Singh landed there in a Beechcraft. In another ten days, the strip was taking Dakota (C-47) transport aircraft.
>
> For the first time in nearly two months, Poonch was again accessible to the rest of the country. This was a great morale booster for the inhabitants—especially as the badly wounded or seriously ill among them could then be evacuated to Jammu. However, there was no great easing of the supply situation. It must be remembered that the airstrip was merely a fair weather runway some 700 yards long constructed by demolishing some barracks, connecting a couple of football fields and filling in a rocky *nullah* bed. At one end was a 30-foot drop to the bed of the Batar: at the other a 10-foot embankment. Dakotas are known to have scraped the heap of dust on the top of the embankment when coming in to land and then just pulled up short of the cliff so that what the pilot could see in front of him was not the runway but the rushing waters of the Batar. As for the surface of the runway, it became dangerously slippery in places and boggy in others after the lightest shower—and showers are not infrequent in those mountainous regions. For all these reasons it was lucky if aircraft could land on the Poonch strip three days in the week, even in the comparatively dry winter season. And since not more than one or two Dakotas could normally be spared for the Poonch run, the average weekly tonnage that could be ferried was about 30-40; together with air-dropped

supplies (on days when the airstrip was "red" but the weather clear) this came to an average of about 50-60 tonnes per week—against a minimum weekly requirement of about 50 tonnes of supplies for the civilian population, 15 tonnes of supplies for the military garrison (at half-rations) and about 15 tonnes of ammunition and stores (at half "contact" rates)—a total of about 80 tonnes.

The Brigade Commander decided, therefore, that the garrison would have to fend for itself as far as food grains were concerned. Thus was conceived the first of a series of "grain operations"—raids on surrounding villages (which had been occupied by tribesmen or other Pakistani raiders) with the object of procuring grain. A company or two of infantry, accompanied by 200-300 or so refugees (to act as guides and porters) would set out at dusk, attack the target village and throw back the enemy—then carry away the stocks of grains that were to be found in abundance in the more prosperous dwellings. Often the actual owners of the houses would be with the refugee party—and would point out all the worthwhile stocks. The column, laden with grain, would return by early morning.

Within a few days of the first aircraft touching down on the Poonch airstrip, the enemy had brought his 3-inch mortars forward-located them in the re-entrants on the southern bank of the Poonch River, south-west of the bridge—and begun to shell the airfield. They would time the barrage so that the shells would begin to burst just as the aircraft was about to land. On the 15th of December a Dakota was damaged by mortar fire in this way.

It was for me a new experience to see how Pritam conducted himself in dealing with the refugees. As far as feeding them was concerned, they were to be treated almost at par with military personnel. When not out on operations, we were all regarded as his workforce, whether it was to work on the airfield or collect supplies from the airdrops or to fetch and carry ammunition and rations to the picquets. Some of us resented this egalitarian treatment; but he discouraged any hierarchical attitudes between soldiers and civilians—at least during the first few critical months. I remember once protesting against his order that for the morning meal each day all available personnel from the military garrison would have to go and feed at the same *langars* that cooked for civilians in the town. (He was trying to induce the locals to eat horse-meat cooked with the coarse gruel of rice and *dal*). He was adamant; if we didn't set an example, how could he expect the poor refugees to obey him? And he added that instead of protesting, I should support his policy by myself offering to partake of the common *langar* fare sometimes. I did!

It wasn't long before the inhabitants of the city and some of the State Forces men and their families began to look upon him as a sort of saviour-saint. I well remember that each morning, as he came down from Moti Mahal Palace, where he lived, to the airfield to survey the progress of work, or to organise collection of air-drops, some of the locals would kneel before him and press their foreheads on the hem of his long flowing *poshteen* (a sheepskin outer garment much in use by officers in the old Frontier Province during the British days). It was inevitable that this kind of mass adoration would eventually affect his personality. It would have required a very special kind of person to resist acquiring a megalomaniacal self-image in those circumstances. I suspect that in time he began to consider himself a surrogate Maharaja of Poonch; but even so, he never displayed the slightest degree of arrogance; and he always considered himself as expendable in battle as any of his troops—as I shall recount.

Pritam did not stand on ceremony; and he readily took me into friendship on first name terms. On arrival at Poonch he had taken over Moti Mahal Palace (the Maharaja of Poonch having gone to live in Dehra Dun) and quartered his battalion in and around the building and grounds of the Palace. He had allotted us Sheesh Mahal, a mile away, formerly the British Residency, when Poonch had been an independent state and since then the residence of a collateral princeling. The State Forces, of course, lived in their own barracks (another half-mile or so distant—grouped around the newlymade airstrip).

Pritam occupied the "royal suite" at Moti Mahal, both as his office and his residence. All the officers of his *ad hoc* Brigade HQ and of 1 Kumaon (CO Lieutenant Colonel Dharam Singh) also lived in Moti Mahal—as did a company or two of Kumaonis in and around verandahs and courtyards on the ground floor.

I was a frequent visitor at Pritam's quarters because he used to consult me for advice on staff procedures, operational reports, appreciations, and like communications to Divisional HQ. He made no bones about the fact that he was a rough-cast, practical solider. Office-room refinements and minor staff duties were not his *forte.* He was entirely secure and had no need to be defensive about his ranker background; but the most remarkable of all his qualities was that, as far as I could discover, he had no trace of communal bias in him—neither pro-Sikh nor anti-Muslim, or any such complex. (He was himself a Sikh).

He was frugal—even austere—in personal habits; and he had no acquisitive mania. After his fall from grace, stories began to circulate that during his stay in Poonch he had appropriated costly items from the Palace such as Persian carpets and items of furniture—and much wealth besides. One report even had it that he had stolen the Poonch family jewels from the treasury in the fort. All such stories were without a grain of truth, I am certain. He was not popular with the officers of his battalion; nor did many of my officers like him; but no one ever suspected or accused him of making away with anything for himself. What he did do, however, was to hand out "trophies" to important visitors from Jammu, as largesse from a "ruler"—a symptom perhaps of his exaggerated self-image as overlord of the demesne. Subsequently, when inquiries were made about missing sporting rifles from the armoury, no one came forward with the truth—but I know of least two that were presented by Pritam as gifts to General Kulwant Singh and Air Marshal Engineer when they visited Poonch.

Meanwhile, Divisional HQ air-ferried the remainder of my Battalion to Poonch on a priority basis. Pritam had given me two weeks to "prove" my Battalion, so to say. Looking back on it, a daunting task it surely was for a young officer with just eight years' service, pitchforked into battalion command in battle—and helped by fledgling company commanders with only three to four years service, none of whom he had met before.

I talked matters over with my officers and we all agreed that two things required to be done: first, we would have to convince our Gurkha soldiers that we Indian officers could lead and sustain them in battle just as well as a their former BOs; and the second requirement was to re-instill in the men the habit of instinctive obedience of orders. The time-honoured method of doing that was a heavy dose of parade-ground drill, which they had not been made to do for years, having been almost constantly on active operations—starting with the Chindits in Burma, followed by counterinsurgency on behalf of Dutch colonialists in Java and Sumatra.

I had taken a great liking to one of the COs of the State Forces —Lieutenant Colonel Hira Nand Dubey—a grizzled veteran many years my senior (he was the elder brother of Udai Chand Dubey, a Sandhurst-trained officer of the Indian Army whom I had known well). One night I invited Hira Nand to our Mess in Sheesh Mahal and asked his advice on many local matters operational and administrative. He was very helpful. Regarding my problem with the Gurkhas, he suggested that I should ask Pritam to be allowed to take my men out on a special operational mission as a *complete battalion.* "Get them into battle soon, under your command," he advised.

I followed this excellent piece of advice and went to see Pritam the very next morning. I had already had the Battalion for two weeks "rehab" training, so Pritam approved my suggestion. He said that in fact he had been planning on an offensive operation across the Batar Nullah (the river flowing from the north, past the civil lines area, into Poonch River in the south). I was to carry it out.

It was an uncomplicated operation as far as planning, deployment and resupply were concerned. We could clearly see our objective, and the route to it, from the high ground behind the civil lines and binocular reconnaissance was all that was necessary. In order to preserve secrecy, I did not allow any patrolling across the river—and we knew from local reports that the enemy were not in great strength anywhere on the ridge, no more than a company's worth in the whole target area.

The State Forces knew of two fording places on the Batar; and Hira Nand promised to help out with a platoon of Dogras to carry loads across the river. As there was no artillery of any sort in Poonch and only a very limited amount of 3-inch mortar ammunition had been airlifted in, it was going to be a straightforward bayonet attack with no battalion or brigade fire-plan. For success I would have to rely on surprise, the bayonet, and an offensive spirit.

It was the latter element that I could not be sure about. The Gorkha is not a demonstrative soul; and I had no idea whether our attempts to impose leadership had had any effect. Man Bahadur the former SM had come back from the Centre as an instant promotee under the Direct Commission scheme (mindlessly) introduced in the newly taken over Gurkha battalions. I had appointed (now) Captain Man Bahadur as a rifle company commander and he had since then given me his trust and confidence. I told him to address all the GOs and senior Havildars and tell them that the Battalion would be disbanded and all Gorkha personnel sent back to Nepal in disgrace unless they proved their worth in the forthcoming battle across the river; and I kept my fingers crossed.

On the eve of the attack we crossed the Batar after some difficulty because of the strong current in waist-deep water; but the approach march by compass was a simple affair. We met no enemy on the way.

My plan was to deploy three companies in line at the assembly area and attack three-up, each company under one of the new Indian officers who would lead the attack. Man Bahadur's company was to be in reserve. I would move with Advance Battalion HQ immediately behind the centre company.

It was a starlit night and we were able to string out in line without a great deal of noise. At 1 o'clock (I think it was) we started the attack. I could see a part of the extended line of the centre company start to advance. The slope was gentle at the foot of the ridge but the gradient became steeper as we climbed higher. When we were about one-third of the way up, shots were fired at us from the top of the ridge. At once every man jack in the leading company lay down on the ground and the advance stopped. I shouted "Get up: advance!" several times and then began to belabour some of the men still lying down with my long walking stick. After a little while, I heard Captain Man Bahadur walk up to me and start to shout at the men. Between us, kicking and prodding them, literally, we eventually got them moving again. There were, of course, no casualties—all the firing was unaimed and random. Not until we neared the top did we suffer two or three men wounded. We had secured the crestline well before first light.

We had "proved" ourselves; after a faltering lapse halfway to the objective, there had been no more hesitation. The final bayonet-charge by the men in front of me had been spirited enough. (The enemy had already withdrawn along the ridge, but our men hadn't known that). At about five o'clock, just before first light, I authorised Adjutant Krishnamurthi to send up the success signal by Verey pistol and also to confirm the message by wireless.

In my verbal orders to my company commanders before the attack I had emphasised the occupation of platoon defensive posts on the ridge immediately after its capture; and to protect them by stone walls (*sangars*) until Kashmiri porters could deliver their meagre loads of barbed wire. I should have checked on this myself, particularly in the company on my right, which was the direction in which the enemy had withdrawn; but the mood was euphoric; and the company commanders had all come in turn to Headquarters to exchange congratulations. We paid for our neglect as soon as it began to get light.

The first indication that our right flank was insecure came when a Bren gun opened up against us, somewhere from a slightly higher feature to the right. Hearing orders being shouted, and much commotion in the right-hand company, I clambered diagonally up the hill towards the crestline, shouting the password as I approached the top. There was much noise, groans from the wounded and signs of indecision—but no panic. Just below the crest three or four bodies had been laid out on the ground; by then there was enough light to see for about a couple of hundred yards—and I realised then that our position was overlooked by a slightly higher feature about that distance away (which should have been reconnoitred before as a priority task). The low stone wall that had been built facing that direction was only one stone deep, with nothing to cover the gaps between the stones. Here I found the company senior GO, an excellent Subedar called Hoshiar Mal, lying with a bullet through his lungs. There were one or two others who were lightly wounded, sticking to their posts. From this I took heart, the Gurkhas were not going to run away. And they never again did, then or ever. (Hoshiar Mal recovered from his wounds but was never able to return to duty).

I told the company commander to send a two or three-man patrol out, downhill beyond the crestline and then, working its way northwards, it should try and locate the enemy base or rear-party. He had already sent men inching to the right along the crest. By then it was light enough for accurate observed shooting but they were pinned down by sniper fire, I told the Company Commander to send runners to order all the section commanders to exercise fire-control and conserve ammunition. (I couldn't see any target to fire at, even through my binoculars).

I walked southwards just under the crestline to my HQ to keep other company commanders informed and to order stretcher-bearers from their companies to the right flank to help carry the dead and wounded back from the crestline.

At about 8 am I visited the right-hand company again. By then it was clear that the forward post was overlooked by the enemy on the higher feature to the right and the slightest movement drew sniper fire from that direction. Furthermore, there was a man lying wounded in the dip immediately to our right—defiladed from the enemy and, therefore, in no further danger of being shot at again; but all attempts to send succour only caused further casualties—which had by then steadily mounted to ten or twelve dead and wounded (as far as I recall). I considered pulling the whole company back about two hundred yards down the ridge where the forward post would be out of effective fire.

Just then a runner came up from Battalion HQ to inform me that the Brigadier was on his way up the hill. I went down the slope to meet Pritam. I have no hesitation in admitting that his presence—unhurried and unperturbed—had a reassuring effect on me and much of my increasing anxiety abated.

When I discussed my plan with him up on the crestline, he didn't agree to any pull-back on my part. It might seem just a readjustment of positions to me, he said, but to the enemy it would seem that they had succeeded in pushing us back; and that wouldn't do. We would have to stick it out where we were—and try and rush the enemy after dark. Meanwhile, he told me to lay out my white Air Indication Panel in a prominent place near the forward post; and he sent a message over his wireless set to ask the IAF in Jammu to rocket the enemy hill on our right.

Our men had doubled the thickness of the *sangar* walls by then, so we crept up to it and I showed him where our wounded scout lay in the dip—about a hundred yards away. Pritam judged that the portion of the intervening ground that was exposed to enemy view was only about twenty yards. He ordered two extra Bren guns to be deployed along the *sangar* wall (which by then had been extended downwards for some distance). He ordered the Brens to give covering fire and asked for two Gurkha riflemen to jump over the wall and rush down to the wounded man.

"Come on Palit, let us help them bring the man back." So saying, he coolly got up and clambered over the wall—leaving me no option but to follow him! Luckily the covering fire proved an effective deterrent.

We got the man back.

That was my first experience of him on a battle-field. It was not the only one, as I shall recount. He seemed to have little regard for personal safety—whether because of a high degree of courage or just insensitivity to fear, I could not tell; but his *reclame* soon spread throughout the Battalion.

In the early afternoon the Air Force came to our rescue in the shape of a lone Spitfire, which after a preliminary reconnaissance pass strafed and rocketed the ridge on our right—effectively stopping the sniping. (Next dawn, after we attacked and captured the enemy post we found three dead bodies in "semi-uniforms").

That just about put a cap on the "Gurkha Ridge" operation. I left a platoon picquet each on the highest point of the ridge and on the pimple overlooking the river, and withdrew the rest of the Battalion to barracks.

The next month or more were spent in a series of minor operations to collect grain from surrounding Suddhan villages. We would go out in two-or-three-company strength escorting a couple of hundred of our refugees, collect grain from the houses and—the following night—escort the porters back to Poonch, picquetting the heights on the way—NWFP fashion.

In mid-February I had to be evacuated to Delhi with jaundice but returned after about six weeks at the MH. By then not only had the Battalion been well blooded, but the company commanders also had got the "feel" of the men. Indian troops, by and large are easy to command and are responsive to discipline—but Gurkhas, we found, were even more so. Obedience, loyalty and courage in battle are almost instinctive; but what they do require is a more intimate interaction with their officers than is the case with most Indian classes.

The first big operation after my return from hospital was a fairly strong Brigade column of about six-company strength, mixed Gurkhas, Kumaonis and Kashmiris, to establish a strong picquet on a feature named Pt 6005 on the map (if memory serves) well to the south of Poonch River, overlooking the valley that led southward to Mendhar. Brigadier Pritam Singh commanded the column himself. I had no particular job to do (but didn't want to be left behind in Poonch, holding the fort) so he left Dharam Singh behind instead and took me along with him as an appendage to his HQ. It was thus that I learned about the sudden panic that engulfed Brigade HQ personnel later that night—and the manner in which Pritam dealt with it.

When the attack on Pt 6005 was being put in I had been left behind with Rear Brigade HQ. The feature was captured without difficulty but soon afterwards the enemy put in a spirited counter-attack. I was told afterwards that a couple of civilian stretcher-bearers (from among the Poonch refugees) dropped their load and ran back, thus starting a sudden panic move backwards. Pritam, I was told, failed to stop them running away, so he promptly pulled out his pistol and shot one of the men as he ran past him—thus stopping the rot. Although I heard the story long after the operation was over, it seemed to be generally known.

Soon after the setting up of a picquet on Pt 5006, the enemy brought up a mountain gun, located it somewhere to the north-west of Gurkha Ridge, and begun to shell the airstrip—especially when Dakotas from Jammu came over to land. In fact one aircraft was hit by shrapnel and had to be left on the airstrip till a repair team could be flown in from Jammu. Pritam determined to expand the ring of picquets once again.

It was decided to evict the enemy from the short ridge sloping from Pt 5724 (the highest point of Gurkha Ridge, captured a few weeks previously by the Kashmir State Forces commanded by Colonel Hiranand Dube). Pritam decided that it was again the Gurkhas who would undertake the operation and again allowed me to take the Battalion out as a whole—(as before, without artillery support). I shall quote again from the Regimental History of the J&K Forces (pages 215-216):

"One of the most spirited actions in Poonch took place on the night of 17/18 May, when 3/9 Gurkha Rifles put in a battalion attack on Pt 4036. The ridge was estimated to have been held by about a company of regular Pakistani troops—though in the event it was found that over 200 enemy were deployed in the area. After a nine-mile night march, the Gurkhas under Colonel Palit began their silent assault up the ridge. Enemy positions were encountered after the first five hundred feet and a running battle ensued. By the time the Gurkhas had reached the top, three successive lines of enemy posts had to be taken at bayonet point. Casualties were unexpectedly heavy (one officer, one JCO and 13 men killed and over 30 wounded— including the CO, Colonel Palit). Next morning, while the wounded were being evacuated, a strong enemy counter-attack was repulsed, but some of the tribesmen took up positions on the lower slopes to the south—where their sniping pinned down the stretcher-bearers carrying the wounded.

That evening, therefore, Colonel Maluk Singh of the Kashmir State Forces was ordered to put in an attack and dislodge the enemy from that spur. 8 JAK with two companies (A and B) set out at 6.00 pm—reaching the assembly area by midnight. Here guides from the 3/9 Gurkhas led the JAK troops to the starting line—and the assault went in at 3.00 am on the 19th May. Complete surprise was achieved: the enemy probably had not expected such prompt reaction from the Poonch garrison. The tribesmen bolted down the far side of the hill leaving behind three dead. Brigadier Pritam Singh, who had also come up to the feature behind 9 JAK, had brought a company of Kumaonis with him. He personally escorted the wounded back to Poonch—a six-hour march downhill and across the fast-flowing waters of the Batar Nullah. By 6.00 am next morning all the wounded were lined up on the airstrip, still on their stretchers, waiting evacuation by air."

I had been wounded when the leading troops had nearly reached the crest, about a hundred feet above us—as far as I could judge in the dark. When being chased up the slope the Pakistanis had kept lobbing grenades downhill over their shoulders. I saw several flashes and heard the explosions ahead of us. As I was up with the leading company, I caught a grenade burst in the chest and face. The grenade must have been one of the locally produced ones, not the British 36 grenades that we had, else there would have been little left of me. As it was, I was suddenly blinded, felt several injuries on my chest, face and stomach, and fell to the ground. About an hour or so later, I was taken down the hill for a few hundred feet and dumped at Battalion HQ where Krishnamurthy applied field dressings on my wounds.

I could vaguely make out the approach of light as dawn broke, but I couldn't see anything in front of me. As it grew lighter, we came under sniper fire from a spur somewhere to the right—but though we could hear the "tak-dum" of tribal rifles, and the bullets smacking into the hillside, we suffered no further casualties. Later in the morning Krish told me that he could see the enemy assembling on a hill above us on a parallel spur, probably for a counter-attack; but the appearance of a lone fighter aircraft above us, though it could not carry out strafing runs in that confused situation, held the enemy at bay. Later in the day, Colonel Maluk Singh came up with two companies of his Battalion (8 JAK) and cleared the enemy from the spur.

When darkness came, our stretchers were taken down the steep slope to the bottom of the ridge. This was an agonising experience, because my body was by then full of aches and pains; and I kept slipping down the stretcher on to the shoulders of the bearer holding the lower end. My morale must have sunk to zero by then—what with being blinded, weak with loss of blood and pain and being "mishandled" down the slope for hours (or so it seemed).

Never was I so glad to hear a voice than when I heard Pritam hailing us when we reached the bottom, asking where the CO Sahib was. He had come for-ward with about fifty Kumaonis to escort the wounded back to Poonch. That was just like him. I felt instantly cheered when I felt his hand grip mine, silently sympathising. One remembers such a moment all one's life.

On reaching Poonch I was carried up to my room in Sheesh Mahal, where Major Sule MC, the Brigade Surgeon, spent a half-hour pulling out bits and pieces of grenade from my body. He told me that the extraction of the bigger pieces would have to be done under an anaesthetic, probably in Delhi. By then I could make out light and dark: and by the time I was loaded on to a Dakota C47 aircraft at the airstrip, I felt greatly reassured because my sight was coming back. I was first evacuated to Jammu; and by the evening flight to the Military Hospital at Delhi Cantt.

My wounds healed quickly and my eyesight was fully restored; so I was able to talk the MS at GHQ (Major General PN Thapar) out of posting me to the IMA for which he had already issued orders. I returned to the Battalion—but not for long. Within a week I received a signal from the MS posting me out of the Battalion "on attachment to Military Training Directorate". I assumed that this was probably an uncoordinated off-shoot from the IMA posting I had circumvented; and I so informed Pritam, who granted me three days leave to go to Delhi and sort it out.

At Army HQ, Delhi, General Kulwant Singh (CGS) told me that I had been selected for a course in the USA, at the Command and Staff School at Fort Leavenworth—and the Ministry had approved it.

I was not about to pass that one up! This was the first vacancy on a training course offered to the Indian Army by the Americans and I rejoiced to have been chosen. However, I obtained permission from the CGS (who, I suspect, had a major say in my selection) to return to the Battalion to say my farewells. I could not make a fly-by-night-exit from my newly "conquered" Gurkhas.

On the flight back to Jammu I sat next to Brigadier Sathe, Commander Artillery of Jammu Division, whom I had met before. I noted that Sathe, in discussing Poonch affairs with me, kept referring to Pritam in derogatory terms. When I bridled at this, he said that he and Pritam had been in the same term at the IMA, where the latter used to be referred to as "Burchha" (or some such belittling term) because of his uncultured ways and his ranker mannerisms; and said that Pritam had been lucky not to have been relegated a term at the IMA—or even totally rejected as being unfit to become an officer.

I angrily told him that no other person I knew could have handled the desperate situation in Poonch during the first few months of its siege. In fact a number of senior Colonels—from Sandhurst and the IMA—had passed up the offer of this promotion. I emphasised that in my opinion, no one else could have rallied the demoralised men of the State Forces and the starving and helpless refugees in Poonch city to work together for the defence of the enclave. Pritam had shown leadership of a high order; and even if he had had to be ruthless on occasion, he had always been just, decisive and personally fearless. To support my case I cited the instance of his shooting down a runaway stretcher-bearer to stop panic at the source. Sathe took it all in and then lapsed into silence.

I said my farewells in Poonch, visited the picquets—both ours and also one or two held by the JAK troops and Kumaonis—and returned to Delhi. My wife and I packed up our flat, sold our Mercedes 170 sports car, surplus furniture and other impedimenta. I made air reservations for my wife and baby daughter, who were to follow me to the States in a couple of weeks. We felt on the top of the world.

On the eve of my departure we were given a farewell dinner at Nirula's by Subroto Mukherjee (a distant family connection—soon to be Air Chief) and his wife Sharda. Halfway through dinner,

Krishen Sibal (formerly of my erstwhile Regiment, The Baluchis) my brother-in-law, called me from his desk at MS Branch to say that General Cariappa, Western Army Commander, wanted to see me urgently. I was to go to his house on King George's Avenue at once.

My first thought was that the General probably wished to congratulate me on my selection. I said my farewells to my host and fellow guests and drove to King George's Avenue.

The General offered me a drink. After he handed it to me I sat down on the couch, as bid. The General—while still pouring himself a whisky, said:

"Palit, I understand you have accused your Brigade Commander of murder!"

The glass of whisky nearly fell from my hand. In a flash I realised what Cariappa was referring to. During my visit to Poonch after a six-week absence, I had picked up the local gossip that the GOC in Jammu, Atma Singh, was a bitter enemy of Kulwant; and also that he was trying to get at Kulwant through his "protégé" Pritam; and in this he had no less an accomplice than the Army Commander, Cariappa, whose antagonism to Kulwant Singh (mutually reciprocated) was well known in the Army.

Cariappa explained that he had had a report from my GOC, Atma Singh, that I had told his Artillery Commander, Sathe, about an incident when Pritam had shot a man—and not reported the incident. Was that true? If so, my statement amounted to a report of murder.

When I recovered from the shock, I explained the circumstances to the General: that I had cited the instance in support of my Brigadier when Sathe had spoken on him in disparaging terms. I felt certain that a man reputed to be fair and righteous man like Cariappa would appreciate the sentiment.

I had first met Cariappa many years previously, during the War, when I was an Instructor Class "C" (Captain) at the Tactical School, Deccan College, Poona. He had just been appointed as the Commanding Officer of an Infantry Battalion, the first Indian officer to be thus promoted (1942, I think). He had been sent for a short attachment to the Tactical School to be instructed on various tactical and organisational aspects of battalion command—and I had been appointed his mentor and Liaison Officer. I had found his affected mannerisms—trying to emulate a British accent and to reflect British mannerisms—somewhat incongruous; but otherwise I had felt great respect for this the most senior of all Indian officers.

In 1947, when I had briefly stayed at the Thimayyas' house on Roberts Road in Delhi (during the Partition communal riots) Cariappa used to be a regular visitor there (before he went off to attend the IDC in London) but, of course, he and I hardly interacted—he being so much older and more senior. Nevertheless, like most Indian officers, I was well aware that Cariappa always tried to mould himself on the model of the upstanding and foursquare qualities of the British officers—impartiality, fairness, and justice.

It was, therefore, with quite a shock that I realised, as Cariappa began a tirade against Pritam Singh, that he was being anything but just and impartial. Clearly, what he was after, was for me to implicate my Commander in a criminal incident.

When I refused to comply, he turned stern and uncompromising. When even that availed nothing, he told me to report to his office at nine o'clock the next morning.

I informed him that I was to catch a plane in the early afternoon to proceed on a course to the USA. He did not react.

"I'll see you at nine", he said, dismissing me.

When I called at his office the next morning, Cariappa had his Assistant Judge Advocate General, Colonel Sen, with him. He said that he wanted me to repeat my story to the AJAG for the record. When I refused to have my story put into writing, Cariappa started to cajole me:

"There is nothing to worry about, Palit. I assure you that we won't use your statement. I want this just as a record, not as evidence." I clearly remember that assurance. Reluctantly I went to Sen's office across the corridor and told him what I had told Brigadier Sathe, which he recorded in his handwriting. I was then allowed to go home for last minute packing.

At mid-day Cariappa sent for me again. As I entered his office, he said:

"You will have to sign this, Palit." He waved the statement at me.

When I asked why, he said that my statement was usable as evidence in a court-martial and that I must sign it!

I was both frightened and angry at this duplicity on Cariappa's part. I reminded him of his assurance to me before I had made the statement, but he brushed that aside.

"Your statement is useable as evidence, so I must have it. You have a plane to catch in a couple of hours. Sign the document—and you can still get to it in time."

I refused; and I added that on no account would I give evidence verbal or written, against my Brigadier. Thereupon the Army Commander *ordered* me to sign the statement. I still refused.

"You'll be sorry for this, Palit. I am going to cancel your course in America." And he picked up the phone, asked for the DMT and did just that.

Cariappa's duplicity and vengeful reaction caused a considerable domestic set-back to the Palits. We had sold most of our household goods, not to mention our precious Mercedes 170 Sports Saloon (which I had bought at a concessional price from the Gwalior garages). We had hoped to replace all of them by purchases in America. We were reduced to living in hardship circumstances at the KER Mess (but fortunately, we did not take immediate steps to replace our belongings).

Cariappa had me in again the next morning. As before, he began by being kind and sympathetic and said that there was still time for me to catch another plane in a day or two—if only I would sign my statement. I had lost respect for him by then, and as happens in the circumstances, my anger was stronger than the awe and fear I had felt before. I told him firmly that it was not my practice to let down my commanders and on no account would I put my signature to the document in question. He then threatened legal action against me. Perhaps over-hastily, I told him that I would resign my commission before I acted according to his wishes.

"All right," he said, not quite believing me. "Bring me your letter of resignation."

Scoring my only point in these exchanges, I told him that as I was still detailed on a course of instruction, I came under the DMT, I would, therefore, take my resignation to the CGS.

I went home, almost in tears, and wrote out my resignation. I did not tell my wife about this decision; there would be time enough later. It was a poignant moment—and I thought of my old father with a heavy heart. He had had very bright hopes of his son when I had followed him into the Service. As for my future, I dared not think about that yet.

I went to Army HQ and straight up to the CGS office. After only a moment's wait in his Military Assistant's office, I was ushered into Kulwant's room.

I told Kulwant the whole story and added that rather than get involved in legal action to make me give evidence at a court-martial, I had decided to resign my commission and go home as a civilian. Kulwant, rightly annoyed with me for being such a blabber-mouth, was nevertheless pleased at my attitude and commended me for having withstood Cariappa's threats.

"All right, Palit. Don't worry about being forced to give evidence, I will see that you don't have to; and I'm tearing up your resignation—you don't have to indulge in any dramatic gestures."

I told him that I had decided to leave the Army only because of Cariappa's threat to prosecute me legally and force me to give evidence.

"Who is Cariappa?" asked Kulwant with his typical flamboyance. "I shall post you in my Branch and see that he can't get at you. Then after its all blown over, I will send you abroad for a couple of years—anywhere you wish to go."

Kulwant kept his word, all the way. He posted me to SD Directorate (G1 SD1, no less!). I was not approached by anyone to give evidence at any Court of Inquiry or Court Martial. Whether any such move was blocked by the CGS, I do not know. "Zoru" Zorawar Singh of the CIH (a term my junior at the IMA) was hurriedly despatched to the Fort Leavenworth Course in my place.

After about ten months in the job, Kulwant sent for me to tell me that he had been planning postings of our first few Military Attaches to our newly opened embassies. I could take my pick!

I consulted my wife. We didn't want to go to Europe, which had not yet started on its way to recover after the devastation of six years of war. America was bespoke (Diloo Chaudhuri—I think). So we chose the glamour centre of the war years—Cairo, which had the advantage that the MA Cairo's purview included a large parish—Ethiopia, Libya, Sudan, Cyprus, Trans-Jordan, Syria and the Lebanon. We left to take up our appointment in July 1949.

One last grace note: Shortly before I left my office at GHQ, Pritam, who had been put up for court martial on various contrived charges, (but not including murder!) walked into my office one afternoon, shook my hand and told me that he had come just to let me know that he knew the whole story of my gaffe. He was convinced that however foolishly I may have spoken, he had not the slightest doubt of my loyalty to a senior and to a friend.

I can't think of many people who would have gone out of their way, as did Pritam, to set someone's mind at rest so effectively.

Appeal for an Unsung Hero

The weak can never forgive. Forgiveness is the attribute of the strong.

—*Mahatma Gandhi*

In 1896, there occurred an incident in France which split the country's public opinion and had far-reaching effects on the French Republic. It was alleged that a Jewish Army officer, Captain Dreyfus, had been convicted and punished by a military tribunal on false charges and forged documents. The famous writer Emile Zola also jumped into the fray with his famous, "I accuse". The matter shook the French nation, and public pressure finally obtained his clemency.

In British India too, there have been such affairs, where Lord Clive and Warren Hastings were accused of serious wrong-doings and fraud. Notwithstanding the many charges against them, they both finally earned an honourable pardon on the strength of their impeccable services to the British Empire.

One is compelled to ask—is there no reprieve or pardon for the 1947–48 Kashmir War's greatest military hero? A man who did no wrong, but was framed by his jealous detractors, based on forged documents and false charges?

Having re-lived the incredible story of Brigadier Pritam Singh, MC, the esteemed reader must introspect. And give serious thought to the pressing need that the Supreme Commander of India pardon this soldier-patriot and restore his honour.

It is quite incredible that more than seventy years after Brigadier Pritam Singh, MC, was sentenced by court-martial, very few people know the real charges against him, or how this brave soldier was wrongly convicted. It is commonly said that "…he stole a carpet from the palace of the Maharaja of Poonch …". While ignorant individuals often repeat this ridiculous accusation, the successes Pritam achieved with his gallant deeds have all too easily been forgotten. Almost wholly obscured are details of how Kashmir and Poonch were won from the raiders and became a part of India, and how Pritam's significant contributions made this a reality!

Today, Brigadier Pritam Singh, MC, India's forgotten soldier-patriot is no more with us. He died some years ago in the anonymity of Punjab's countryside, with no mention in the newspapers. Sadly, India's greatest military hero of the First Kashmir War died a forlorn and neglected man, without the country's media writing even a two-line obituary about him and his great deeds for his motherland.

May the Indian nation remember his great deeds as a soldier-patriot and may the President of India be gracious to pardon and belatedly honour him for his brave deeds.

> *"… I have done my duty to India and one day the truth will be out for all to see."*
>
> *—Brigadier Pritam Singh, MC.*

Brig Pritam Singh, MC in his last days

Appendix I

Operation Pooonching

Excerpts from Operation Pooonching, Shiv Kunal Verma (Vayu 2000 Aerospace Review, printed with permission of the author)

...

Recollects Air Marshal Grewal, "We did move our troops into Poonch but soon after they were totally cut off as Pakistan had completely surrounded the valley from all sides and the only way in was by air. There was no airfield as such though there was a small level place available where horses used to be exercised. On one side there was the river, with a steep drop of a hundred odd-feet, while on the other there was a hut. The total length of the field was some 600 yards. Landing an aircraft there under any circumstances would have been very difficult but at that time we had an extremely capable leader....Air Commodore Mehar Singh. But for him, I think that the operations would have been quite impossible for the Air Force."

Brigadier Pritam Singh was "a tough guy", and one who was to display remarkable courage and determination in the days to come. To facilitate a regular flow of supplies, not only for the Poonch Brigade but also for the 10,000 locals and 35,000 refugees, Brigadier Pritam Singh organised hundreds of refugees to construct an improvised airstrip.

Pritam Singh and Mehar Singh were symbolic of the determination and courage of the armed forces which had to coordinate to save Poonch. Prime Minister Nehru had declared that Poonch would be saved "at all costs". Kotli had already been relieved by Indian troops advancing from the south, but the advance was also temporarily halted at that stage. Around Poonch, the Indian pickets were well sited to meet the threat of the raiders from all sides. Based at Jammu, RIAF Tempest fighter-bombers and Harvards attacked enemy positions. On December 4th, Tempests subjected enemy positions north-east and northwest of Poonch to 20mm cannon fire and again on December 7th, enemy positions in the immediate vicinity of Poonch were subjected to rocket attack and strafing.

On December 8th, a Dakota successfully dropped supplies and an improvised aircraft bombed enemy targets north of Poonch while on December 9th, supplies of ammunition were dropped. Recalls Air Marshal Grewal, "At night the raiders used to move their convoys around freely because during the day Tempests would harass them repeatedly, inflicting heavy losses. Mehar Singh then had this bright idea . . . why not load a bomb into the cargo compartment of a Dakota aircraft and roll it out of the door. So we began to do just that, live-fusing in the aircraft with a torch and rolling it out. The bomb could land anywhere within the radius of half a mile, but it created a big bang...and the man on the ground did not know where it was going to land either."

It took the refugees, toiling under hostile mortar fire, six days to complete the Poonch landing strip, with fighters providing cover overhead. According to Desmond Pushong's log book, he first flew into Poonch, from Jammu, in a Harvard with Flying Officer Choudhry on December 10th. Says he, "I went to take a look and familiarise myself with the terrain. Two days later, Mehar Singh landed the Harvard there also and followed that with a Dakota landing. At Jammu he told us that it was a difficult task but it could be done. All of us were very keen to get going and I landed there for the first time on December 12th."

Pushong's crew consisted of Fg Offrs Menon, Roy and WO Nanu, flying the Dakota II (VP 903). It was soon to become a familiar aircraft for the Poonch garrison. Yet another Dakota was hit while air dropping ammunition but managed to land safely at Poonch.

On December 13th, VP 903 landed at Poonch on three occasions during the day. But it was premature for the Indians to celebrate. The raiders moved up field guns and by the evening had the airfield brack-eted by mortars and field artillery. Recalls Wg. Cdr. Pushong, "After having got there in the first place, there was now this new crisis. I was at the bar in the mess when Mehar Singh walked in and he called Grewal and me aside. He asked the two of us if we were willing to fly there again with these howitzers and land at Poonch at night without any lights. I said we could try. His only brief to us was that if we found ourselves overshooting the runway, we were to retract our undercarriage! Anyway, Grewal said we would get the guns there but he joked that the squadron might be minus two Dakotas. Mehar Singh just looked at us and said that was acceptable."

The 3.7" howitzers were from the right section of the 4th (Hazara) Mountain Battery (F.F.). After loading, the two Dakotas took off on a bright moonlit night. Mehar Singh was hoping that the enemy gunners would have covered their guns and would be asleep. Air Marshal Grewal takes up the story, "I was to land first but our Pushong never listened to any briefings and he just cut me out and landed first, so I had to do a holding circuit behind the hills and wait."

On the ground the first Dakota had barely come to a halt when a Kumaoni officer hauled himself abroad. Pushong grabbed his *khukri* and they slashed the ropes with which the guns were tied, the waiting troops manhandling the guns onto the airstrip. Within minutes, VP 903 was airborne again. "There was no breeze and as the airstrip was a Kutcha place, dust was hanging over it after Pushong took off. I couldn't wait too long and as a result I think it was the most stupid landing I ever did. I got to the threshold and cut the engines, but I couldn't see. I was just hanging there, hoping the aircraft would touch down. Minutes later, we had cut the second gun loose and were off again...I was just getting off the ground when the enemy firing started." But now the besieged Poonch garrison had got its own howitzers.

Appendix II

Interaction between Brigadier Jasbir Singh and Naib Subedar Bhim Singh

In July 2019, I interacted with a 98-year-old veteran named Naib Subedar Bhim Singh of 1 Kumaon (Para), who had flown to Srinagar in October 1947 and fought at Shalateng and Poonch under Brigadier Pritam Singh, MC. Despite his advanced age, Bhim Singh was coherent and articulate, and remembered most of the events of 1947–48 quite clearly. However, sometimes he would lapse into an unintelligible garble, and I had to gently coax him back to the present time. The interaction provided valuable details of the brave men and the gallant actions they took to save Kashmir and Poonch for India, more than seventy years ago:

Naib Subedar Bhim Singh

Naik Bhim Singh

[Author] What is your name and what are your personal particulars?

[Bhim Singh] I am number JC 27828, Naib Subedar Bhim Singh. My father was Bhagwan Singh and I was born on 6 May 1923 at Village Khania, Tehsil Ranikhet, District Almora. My wife is Laxmi Devi and she is still alive. I have two sons and a daughter. I joined the Army (1 Kumaon) during World War II and fought in both Middle East and Indonesia (Java) against the Germans and Japanese forces. After the War, my battalion returned to India and it was converted to a parachute unit. We did our jumps at Chaklala, I think, in undivided India and I received my "parachute wings".

With the author on 21 July 2019

[Author] Who was your Commanding Officer (CO)?

[Bhim Singh] I do not remember his name, but he was a "gora".

[Author] Was this your CO (after showing him a photo of Lieutenant Colonel GB Beer)?

[Bhim Singh] Yes, yes (with a smile), he was the CO. He was relieved at Delhi by a Sikh officer named Lieutenant Colonel Pritam Singh. He was the unit's first Indian CO, and he flew with us to Kashmir.

[Author] Tell me about your move from Delhi to Kashmir and the actions that you fought on the way to Poonch.

[Bhim Singh] Two companies and Battalion HQ flew out early in the morning from Willingdon Airport, while it was still dark. I was a Naik and part of "D" Company and had two stripes on my sleeve. The other companies flew in later. We landed at Srinagar Airfield at about 9 AM and quickly unloaded the plane. We loaded our gear onto the civilian buses and lorries that had been provided for us and moved to Srinagar. On the way there was an encounter with the Raiders and the unit suffered some casualties. However, my vehicle was not involved in the fighting. Later, we moved to Shalateng, near Srinagar, and clashed with the Raiders. CO gave us orders to open fire. Armoured Cars also opened heavy automatic fire from our left side. Most of the Raiders were killed in the ploughed field due to our heavy firing. Bombs and machine-gun bullets were fired from two of our aircraft and that destroyed most of the Raiders' buses and lorries on the road. The surviving Raiders ran away along the main road. We went to the field and searched the dead Raiders. There were nearly 600 dead Raiders lying in heaps in the field.

After some time, vehicles arrived for us. We loaded up and moved behind the fleeing Raiders. Our vehicles were led by two Armoured Cars. On the way we came under heavy fire at Mahura, where the Raiders had stopped to destroy the power station. We got off and attacked the Raiders, who fled down the road. The power station had been saved. We again followed the fleeing enemy. At Uri we left the main road and turned "left". After travelling some distance on a smaller road, we came under heavy fire. Many casualties were suffered in the vehicle before us. Some Raiders destroyed a large wooden bridge by setting it on fire and the road. We attacked and the Raiders fled. A diversion was made and we could get across the nullah.

We cut branches from surrounding trees and cremated bodies of the soldiers who had been killed in the engagement. Then, we moved on and entered Poonch. We had been delayed considerably by the incident. Poonch was like a "ghost-town" when we entered, as the people were very scared. They were hiding in their houses and we could see them carefully watching us from behind their windows. There were two understrength State Force battalions in Poonch. Their Muslim soldiers had deserted earlier and the battalions were ready to leave Poonch. Our CO stopped them from leaving and they joined us to fight the Raiders, who were camped on the hills around the town.

[Author] Tell me of your time in Poonch.

[Bhim Singh] After we had entered Poonch, the Raiders closed the track by which we had come from Uri. We were thus, surrounded in Poonch for about the next one year. During this time, we repeatedly defended Poonch and drove back the enemy. Along with the civilians, we constructed an airfield next to the town and alongside Betaar Nala. There were also thousands of refugees in the town, who had converged from neighbouring areas to save themselves from the cruelty of the Raiders. With the help of Pakistan Army the Raiders moved artillery guns on the hills around Poonch and began to shell us and the newly-constructed airstrip, as well. Soon, the CO had guns flown in, and we also began to shell the Raiders. This action by us made the enemy stop his firing of artillery and they also withdrew their artillery guns.

In Poonch we were always very short of food. The added population of thousands of refugees further affected the town's shortage of rations. Once we had to manage with greatly reduced rations, almost no food at all for a complete month. CO used to send our patrols to raid the neighbouring villages and collect grain. Once we even harvested the standing crop, for some grain in return. That is how all were fed in the town.

The CO used to stay in the Maharaja's palace and we often mounted a guard at the palace. A Gurkha unit joined us at Poonch. Later, our unit CO changed and Major Dharam Singh assumed command of the unit. The last CO was promoted to rank of Brigadier, and he took over the Poonch Garrison. Our unit was moved out of Poonch by air.

We came from Jammu and attacked and captured a large hill feature called Pir Badesar after a very tough fight. I was then the Signal Havildar. The CO did a good job and was awarded a Mahavir Chakra (MVC). There were other awards as well.

[Author] Tell me about Lieutenant Colonel (later Brigadier) Pritam Singh, MC?

[Bhim Singh] CO Sahib was an upright man and a brave soldier. He was a good CO, and he commanded the unit well during a very difficult time. He was also a very patriotic man. I have heard he would often talk about ensuring that India defeats all forces sent by Pakistan.

[Author] What do you feel about what later happened with Brigadier Pritam Singh?

[Bhim Singh] Sahib, I do not know very much as we had moved out of Poonch. But I heard that he was tried by a court martial and unfairly punished. It is very bad to wrongly punish a straight-forward and brave man. As you have said, even though he is dead he rightly deserves a pardon. May my CO Sahib get justice, before I die! Ram Ram Sahib.

Farewell Nb Sub Bhim Singh

Prtiam's bust in Poonch

About Authors

Brigadier Jasbir Singh, SM was a retired Indian Army officer from the Kumaon Regiment. He was wounded during operations behind enemy lines in East Pakistan (1971 war) and twice decorated for gallantry during operations. After having served for 34 years in the Army, he led a retired life in the hills of Ranikhet and spent his time writing on military subjects and painting. He authored seven books and numerous articles. His father, Brigadier Balbir Singh, MC was also from the Kumaon Regiment who had escaped from a Japanese POW Camp in Singapore during World War II, along with Parab and Pritam as mentioned in this book. Brigadier Jasbir Singh passed away in April 2022.

Pankaj P Singh is a software engineer turned entrepreneur working in the "Book Industry" for the last twenty-six years. He and his wife together run The Browser, a bookstore and publishing house based in Chandigarh, and proudly serve numerous military formations across the country. Having ventured into publishing in 2018, with a focus on military history through the Fauji Days *(faujidays.com)* platform, this is the third published, and first co-authored, book by him. An avid reader, when not engaged in the world of books and writing, programming in Python keeps his creative juices flowing.

Fauji Days Military Classics

On War
General Carl Von Clausevitz
ISBN: 978-93-92210-13-6

Hira Singh
Talbot Mundy
ISBN: 978-93-92210-09-9

Generals Die in Bed
Charles Yale Harrison
ISBN: 978-93-92210-44-0

Three Soldiers
John Dos Passos
ISBN: 978-93-92210-14-3

War Is a Racket
Smedley D Butler
ISBN: 978-93-92210-15-0

The Red Badge of Courage
Stephen Crane
ISBN: 978-93-92210-16-7

Fauji Days Oral History

More From Fauji Days

Military Pensions Simplified:
Commentary, Case Law & Provisions
Navdeep Singh
ISBN: 978-93-92210-06-8

Gyan Chakra on India's Military Strategy
Edited by Major General Amarjit Singh
ISBN: 978-93-92210-18-1

The Crossover Girl & Other Stories
Ashok Ahlawat
ISBN: 978-93-92210-22-8

Pick of the Army: Guns, Gunners and Mules
The Indian Mountain Artillery, 1851–1985
Lieutenant General NS Brar
ISBN: 978-93-92210-20-4

Drummers Call:
An Anthology of Writings While Following the Drum
Lieutenant General NS Brar
ISBN: 978-93-88150-00-2

Engineering the Victory March:
Bangladesh Liberation War 1971
Brigadier RB Singh
ISBN: 978-93-92210-03-7

The General Called Tsunami: Memoir of a Sapper
Lieutenant General BS Dhaliwal
ISBN: 978-93-92210-05-1

Dusk over the Mustard Fields
Ranjit Powar
ISBN: 978-93-92210-21-1

Other Titles From The Browser

Ekarat: Stories He Left Behind
ISBN: 978-93-92210-08-2

Mahroks: The Story of the Kambojas, Sikhs and Shaheeds
Jewan Deepak
ISBN: 978-93-5737-645-7

The Nightingale and Other Stories
Maniki Deep
ISBN: 978-81-94954-27-9

In and Out of Step
GS Aujla, IPS (Retd)
ISBN: 978-93-88150-17-0

Sociopreneur: Zero to One
Kunal Nandwani
ISBN: 978-93-88150-11-8

Wilderness Is Us: Hiking, Thriving and Learning in the Great Outdoors
Vipul Negi
ISBN: 978-93-88150-07-1

Because Time Does Not Heal
Sahar Gharachorlou
ISBN: 978-93-92210-10-5

Twice Born
Sahar Gharachorlou
ISBN: 978-93-88150-12-5

Wall Paintings: The Vanishing Treasure
Ram Pratap Verma
ISBN: 978-93-88150-15-6